Oh, You Behave!

Social Media Etiquette for Career and
Business Branding Success

MARJORIE JANCZAK

iUniverse, Inc.
Bloomington

Oh, You Behave!
Social Media Etiquette for Career and Business Branding Success

iUniverse books may be ordered through booksellers or by contacting:

iUniverse
1663 Liberty Drive
Bloomington, IN 47403
www.iuniverse.com
1-800-Authors (1-800-288-4677)

ISBN: 978-1-4759-3270-6 (sc)
ISBN: 978-1-4759-3272-0 (hc)
ISBN: 978-1-4759-3271-3 (ebk)

Printed in the United States of America

iUniverse rev. date: 08/01/2012

CONTENTS

Dedication

I humbly dedicate this book to:

All my dear social media and social networking friends—
you all are the inspiration behind this book.

ADVANCE PRAISES FOR
OH, YOU BEHAVE!

Testimonials***

This well-written book is packed with valuable advice for those seeking to '*take on*' the Social (and professional) Media scene. Marjorie's friendly, no-nonsense tips are for both the novice and experienced professional. Whether your company is a highly caffeinated startup, a small gift boutique, or a large law firm, good manners on the Internet are important because they emphasize your willingness to control your behavior for the benefit of others. So, do the right thing and read *Oh You Behave! Social Media Etiquette for Career and Business Branding Success* today so that you can brand yourself appropriately!

—Sue Fox, Author of *Business Etiquette for Dummies*
(Wiley & Son's Inc. 2009)

If you are interested in mastering the art of influencing others online with professionalism and integrity, Marjorie Janczak's Social Media Etiquette Book is an invaluable resource. Her tips, techniques, and advice will empower you and those you interact with to elevate self-esteem and create the strong relationships that are so essential for manifesting success.

—Dr. Joe Rubino, Founder, CenterForPersonalReinvention.com,
Creator, TheSelfEsteemBook.com

Marjorie is a truly gifted woman. An advocate and educator for helping people understand useful etiquette in Social Media.

—Alex Karis
http://www.hurricaneofgratitude.com

Putting "social" in social media and networking is exactly what Marjorie Janczak teaches you in her newest book, Social Media Etiquette for Career and Business Branding Success. Marjorie shows you exactly how to be who you are and shine through with social media. The best part of all is all of her information is based on her personal journey through the social media maze. Standing head and shoulders above others Marjorie's information is a must have for anyone who wants to succeed. There is no hype in her book. Rather, it's all great information that is as good as it gets. Get it today.

—Kathleen Gage
The Street Smarts Marketer
www.kathleengage.com

When I think about social media etiquette I immediately think about Marjorie. I know of no other person who has compiled such a comprehensive book on 'social media' etiquette. Not only does she provide the reader with the etiquette and protocol of social media networking; which is a daunting task when you consider platforms like Facebook, Tweeter and LinkedIn which are in a constant state of change, but also empowers you with the grace and charm to create the right professional image and to step up your game for more success in your career or business networking. Marjorie shares her knowledge of the practical use of various tools that will give any professional a handle on the management of their 'Social Media Networking' empire. With Marjorie's guidance any entrepreneur or career professional can establish a world presence on line with the confidence and self assurance that they are 'socially' correct.

—Walethia Aquil
CEO of Grace and Charm
Creator of the Grace and Charm Success System
www.graceandcharm.com

Marjorie is a tireless guiding spirit, inspiring professionals to give and be their best in all endeavors. She provides salient insights and straightforward advice to help navigate the nuances of social media for appropriate networking, by effectively employing best practices.

—Becky Cortino
Marketing-Communications Indie Pro

ACKNOWLEDGMENTS

This book would not have been written and made available without the motivation and support of a few people who certainly are worth mentioning and acknowledging.

My Big (virtual) Bro Jim Turner, a very influential thought leader in social media. Thank you Jim for being a GREAT big Brother although we have not met physically yet you treat me like your true sister. Thank you also for seeing this book in me and pointing it right out to me right from our early days of meeting. I cannot thank you enough for being so caring and thoughtful.

My great friend Ali Kahn of the Good Advice Group. You also found a book in me even before I could think of one. Thank you too for supporting Jim in making sure that I got this book out.

My dear Amy Wong of Net Directives. Thank you for pointing out my talent to me and encouraging me to write this particular book.

This book would also not be complete without the mention of Bret Griswold. You have shown that distance does not make any difference when it comes to authentic friendship. Your love, kindness, care and support is unbelievable. Thank you for being who you are.

To Sue Fox, my mentor and friend, for using your etiquette experience and professional eyes to analyze this book. Your loving kindness is always appreciated.

Marjorie Janczak

To Lynne Klippel for giving me your writer and publisher's opinion on the book. I very much appreciate it.

And finally, my very good friends Charles Nsenga and <u>Val Waldeck,</u> for handling the fine details with such love and care and for helping me to finish this book. Thank you very much my good friends.

I cherish you all!

About The Author

Marjorie Janczak (pronounced—Yan-shak), also known as The Etiquette Diva, is a Small Business Brand Marketing Strategist and The Preferred Lifestyle Ambassador.

Her passion is to empower independent service professionals—especially women and the minority—who are open to taking a different strategic move and necessary steps that will lead them to get profitably branded to captivate, convince and convert their ideal prospects into paying clients so that they can bank their brilliance and live their preferred lifestyle.

She is the Founder and creator of The Etiquette Equities E-Course, The Power Of YOU! tele-summit, The Six Figure Branding Secrets tele-summit and the Profitably Branded Blueprint Program.

As a host, Marjorie has interviewed over 50 internationally recognized experts on human potential and business development issues. These experts include Joe Sugarman, the marketing marverick; Dr Joe Rubino, the self-esteem guru; Mr Guy Finley; Paul Lawrence Vann; Brad Yates; Dr Joe Vitale and Marci Shimoff of the movie "The Secret."

Mr Alex Karis, a credible social media celebrity calls Marjorie ". . . truly gifted woman. An advocate and educator for helping people understand useful etiquette in Social Media."

Marjorie uses her expertise to help business owners, career oriented people and independent professionals leverage the power of business etiquette and effective communications strategically to profitably brand themselves, make a difference on their bottom line and in their lives.

Marjorie believes "The best wealth you can ever achieve in life is your ability to deal with people." So the better you can master your communications and etiquette as well as your career, the better you will prosper.

This wisdom she gathered is attributed to her wide travels to countries including Togo, Benin, Cote d'Ivoire, Senegal, South Africa, Britain, Scotland, Holland, Germany, Austria and The Americas among others.

Prior to establishing her own business entreprises, Marjorie garnered over 10 years of communications, marketing and etiquette experience in such diverse industries as the Petroleum and Energy, Airline, Non-profits, Property and Publishing mainly in Africa and Europe. These include countries like Ghana, United Kingdom and Germany.

Marjorie holds a Post Graduate in Communications and is also a certified etiquette expert. She is also very avid in social networking and social media.

On a personal note, Marjorie was born to a diplomatic family where good manners and etiquette was not a choice but a MUST.

She is the wife of a loving German with whom she enjoys the company of their two energetic children.

One of their favorite times is helping their mother (Marjorie) in the kitchen and enjoying one of her passions of experimenting new dishes that most of the time turn out to be very much worth the effort.

Want To Know Even More About Me? Then Let's Stay In Touch!

Learn more about how to get profitably branded by visiting:
http://www.profitablybranded.com

Connect with me at:

Twitter:
http://www.twitter.com/MarjorieJanczak

Facebook:
http://www.facebook.com/Marjorie.Janczak

Also don't forget to claim a special gift I've reserved for you by going to:
http://www.ohyoubehave.com/bookgift.html

Or simply drop me an email at:
marjorie (at) ohyoubehave.com

INTRODUCTION

From my experience, the social world is a very open and plain field globally for anyone willing to be there. It can either make or break you depending on how you use it. The word "FREEDOM" is clearly spelled out there. You may call it the virtual playground or even better, the virtual continent. Yes, it is all about social media and social networks!

Hardly had it become well known than some politicians realized its potential and started leveraging it. Many business men and women have also leveraged its power. Organizations, including non-profit ones, have done the same and individuals with or without a potent message have also successfully used it to make their voices heard and created powerful brands globally.

Right at the beginning of 2007 or possibly earlier, a friend of mine (a relationship expert) started a careful research and analysis of these media and built a whole business around this platform. Since then, she has made a fortune each year and created a powerful brand for herself as a social media expert. In fact in 2008, Fast Company dubbed her "the Pied Piper of the online world."*

President Barack Obama surrounded himself with the right professionals and leveraged these platforms to his political advantage. The result was land-slide victory and jubilation of a large section of Americans and a multitude of other people around the world. He confidently entered the White House as the first black American to win the presidential elections.

In October 2008, the parents of a 22-month-old baby girl in England used one of these platforms to search for a bone-marrow donor for their little daughter. Her doctor had diagnosed her with Leukemia and she was approaching death. Almost 7000 potential donors responded to the plea to help this innocent girl. After just two weeks, the right donor was found in Australia.

All these platforms are social media and social networking sites like *facebook, twitter, LinkedIn, google+, Pinterest, Youtube, Tumblr, Digg, Klout, Xing, Ning, Delicious, Technorati, Instagram* and countless others. They have done a great job of bringing people of all walks of life together as well as making communication and necessary information easily accessible, something that was unbelievable a few decades ago.

Different people from all the continents, young and old, have joined in. More are joining daily. Some just want to have their voices heard; others just want to feel "cool". Businesses and professionals are curious as to what this is all about and how it works for business profit, promotion of their products, services and brands. The list doesn't end here. Pressure groups, non-profit organizations and other help-seekers—not forgetting our dear politicians—vigilantly watch as they try to figure out how to use these media to their advantage. Even long-lost friends, classmates and loved ones have been found on these platforms!

But how can professional or business people stand out and attract the ideal personalities in order to succeed on these social media and social networking sites in the midst of millions of users who may be asking for the same thing they are providing?

You, as a professional focused on making profit in your business, might often have said "people are not buying". "this social media is a waste of time". You may be familiar with statements like: "you must have something to give out for free to capture leads and prospective buyers", "you must be seen and heard a lot on as many platforms as possible", "be present and contribute to the conversations", "you must strategically promote your business", and so on. Yes, I also kept hearing them and did my best to do as the 'gurus' said.

However, much as all of these clichés above may be realities, there's a big question mark at the end of each statement. You see, it might be true that people are not buying but why are they not? The fact is that people surely buy things they want regardless of the economic circumstances.

The following might raise voices in some quarters but I have come to confidently conclude that your overall brand strategy plus your total marketing strategy together with how you treat people determines the quality of success you attain!

Building relationships in this world of web 2.0 and 3.0 is so inevitable and important that, as a professional, you have to rethink the relationship with your existing and potential clients. As an entrepreneur, how you relate to the friends you make on the social networking sites is very important in portraying your personal and professional brand—two essential components of your existence as a professional in our world today.

In the world we live in today, people want to do business with those they like, trust and feel comfortable with. Incidentally, these social networking sites are changing the way business is done by providing the platforms to build trust in ourselves and our businesses. This means that it is now even easier and more cost-effective for you to attract the right people and target audience to your business.

For a business relationship to work, both the professional and the client or customer must get value, and that is basically what social media advocate. The relationship will otherwise not last long if it is only one-sided or half-hearted. Luckily enough, these media make it even more affordable—and most times without any charge—to build those valued relationships you need for your business growth and profit.

As a professional seeking to maximize profits in your business, it is in your own interest to find ways and means to cut down costs. As my marketing mentor Dan Kennedy says, ". . . any idiot can build up a business—and many idiots have—using up millions of dollars of stockholders' equity in the process. Genius is in getting customers and making sales without having to use up a huge chunk of capital to do it."

That is exactly what it is all about if you want to leverage the social media platforms for your business success. These social media and networking sites are platforms that small business professionals can leverage at a very minimal or no cost at all.

So how can you use them to achieve success in your business, considering they are mainly "SOCIAL" media although some are business oriented? In fact, I know most of the sites will ban you from using their platform if they realize you are aggressively promoting your business.

This is precisely the reason for writing this book—to help you understand that it is not all about the technology, how many social networks you join, how many friends you are able to make or how well you interconnect all the media together to have a great presence. It is all about how you master the art of building quality mutually beneficial relationships—not just another brand but a profitable and successful business . . . And that is very doable when you take the first step with proper etiquette!

Chapter 1

WHAT EXACTLY IS SOCIAL MEDIA?

Basically, social media is the umbrella for all the virtual interactions we make that have now been made possible by technology. Examples are the sharing of videos and images, audio-files, documents, texts and all forms of social interactions you can think of. We now easily have conversations with various groups of people we formerly had difficulty making contact with.

I recently joined my secondary school year-group "LOSA" on *facebook* and I am so happy and grateful because I had been thinking about some classmates for years and wondering how they are doing. Thanks to *facebook*, I now have contact with them again and we reminisce those good old times.

With tools that the internet provides us, the typical one-way communication that existed between corporations and their customers or clients has been advanced to a two-way communication. Corporations cannot afford NOT to listen to their target audience if they want to have dominance in their market and to get profitably branded. This is what social media in the nutshell is all about.

It does not mean that there are no longer barriers and issues when it comes to corporate and customer communications. Of course there still are! However, in as much as those barriers have been scaled down to allow the customer or client to have some power, the business world, including big corporate conglomerates, cannot avoid paying attention.

In an interview by Geert Lovink with Herbert Schiller, author of "Information Inequality"—he reiterated the fact that George Gilder's belief that the old mass-media monopolies will soon crumble because of the empowering possibilities of individuals by the so-called interactive many-to-many media is not so much the case in reality.

According to Mr. Schiller, "All one could do is look around. Do you see any indications? The monopolies are stronger than ever and the concentration continues. It now embraces a wide area; it is not just 'media'. All forms of communication are brought together in these unified corporate conglomerates. You have Time-Warner, which has assets of about 20 billion dollars and is operating radio stations, recording studios, film studios, television programming and increasingly also retail stores, where they sell the apparels that they produce in their movies . . . To think that these are crumbling is like being in a phantasm-land."

Schiller continues to say that "We have to be careful in using the word 'globalization' in this context. It may seem that everybody is participating in it and you will have to, and if you don't you will fall behind and lose, we have to be competitive, etc. Globalization is a direction of super corporations. They are using the globe to market their products and penetrate every part of the world. But there is a big difference between what they are doing and the whole world population."

As a result, those smart companies who realize the power of the social media are leveraging them to their advantage for more profits, brand awareness and wiping out competition. Great, right?!

The ability to interact where it was impossible before has been facilitated by Web 2.0 (and more recently Web 3.0) which simply means that websites now not only give you information but also allow you to interact on that very site and page on which the information is given. Some social media tools that help with this are **wibija** and **social bookmarks**.

If you visit a site and like what you see or read for example, it should be possible (if the owner has up-to-date technology) for you to 'share' that information with your friends by simply clicking a button on that very page. You should be able to let the owner know that you 'like' the site, again by clicking a button. You should be able to comment on the topic being addressed or discussed either by simply typing or even posting a video of your opinion and a lot more. Some social media sites and tools you might want to look at as an entrepreneur to see how you can leverage their power for your business advantage are blogs, microblogs, photos and video sharing sites, social news, Wikis and—of course very inevitably—social networking.

So here are some detailed explanations to all these:

A blog is the short form for a web log. Examples of blogs and blogging platforms are Wordpress and Typepad. I personally call blogs the advanced websites that are friendly and can talk. This is because a blog is basically a website that you can log on to and have it updated anytime you want. In updating, the posts are displayed in a reversed chronological order so that you have the most recent posts appearing on top of the list. But not just that; people who read your blog posts are able to give their comments on what they think about your blog generally and your post in particular. This enables them (if you have the necessary applications and plugins) to share it with their friends thus spreading your post far and wide beyond your imagination to reach a multitude of potential customers and clients. In this way, you have the potential to spread your messages like wildfire and to ultimately get profitably branded!

Wordnetweb describes a blog as a shared on-line journal where people may post diary entries about their personal experiences and hobbies. Blogs have now become a very powerful medium for businesses to reach their target audiences. So if you are running a business and do not have a blog, I highly recommend you get information on blogs and have one set up immediately for you and your business.

A blog or a social networking site is one kind of Web 2.0. But now let's look further at what social networks are, since I will mainly focus on them.

When it comes to microblogging, the most outstanding tool (if there really are any others at all that can compare) is *twitter*! Without a plan, all the social media tools can become overwhelming for a professional. It so happens that twitter is one platform that can easily confuse you to such an extent that you simply give it up or mess up very badly. Certainly not a good way to get profitably branded.

This is because unlike social networking platforms, twitter generally allows you to send a message or broadcast of no more that 140 characters. This means that as a professional, you must really send a very concise, catchy and meaningful message if you want to catch the eye of any potential follower. Luckily, due to further advancements, there is now the possibility of also sending longer messages on twitter.

Some tools that make the twitter experience fun, more personal and manageable are *tweetdeck*, *socialoomph* and *hootsuit* to mention but a few. In my opinion, it is unprofessional and inhuman to only have your tweets automated, a tactic some professionals use. That certainly is not the right way to build quality relationships. What is more, it is generally only 140 characters so why solely depend on automation? Due to this limitation in characters, it is advisable to know some internet jargons, acronyms and certain words to be able to put enough words in your messages and broadcasts.

Messages and broadcasts sent on twitter are called 'tweets' and as a professional, you would be making a big mistake if you underestimated the power of your tweets. You might think you were talking to everyone and no one in particular, but evidence proves that it has the power to catapult careers and businesses in very cost-effective ways, more so than most media.

No man is an island on his own and we all need people to help us in achieving anything in our lives. Especially as a professional or business person, success in your career is mostly determined by the quality of the people you surround yourself with and the way you deal with the people you interact and collaborate with.

It is an illusion to believe that only your expertise and experience can take you and your career to the next level. For that reason, you would want to consider using at least two of the social networking platforms to follow up on potential partners, clients, suppliers, advisers, you name it. And this would include twitter. These are the people who will make your career or business successful.

Through your tweets, you can gradually find out what people need and—with a little creativity—see how best your expertise can be the solution to their problems. This leads us gracefully to the next item, that is, how you can promote and market your business and expertise on twitter.

However, promotion and marketing must not be your primary aim because it will back-fire in the long-run. Concentrate rather on being a valuable source of information and advice, freely giving advice where necessary as well as gradually paving your way to expert status and eventually becoming a thought-leader. Again, unlike social networking, people can follow you on twitter but you are not obliged to follow every Tom, Dick and Harry.

Then there are the social photo and video sharing platforms like *Flickr*, *Vimeo* and *YouTube*. These are just a few of the many great tools available for you to share images and videos online with others. These tools not only allow people to see your pictures and videos, but also allows them to share their comments. This makes it very interactive and more interesting. It is like sharing a picture or video with your friends and making your comments there and then as you see them instead of having to send an e-mail. You know exactly what picture or video is being talked about and you—the owner of the picture or video—can also comment back in response or join in the discussions about them.

Social news platforms like *Newsvine, Reddit, Digg* and *Propeller* can be very handy for you as a professional. Not only do they keep you up-to-date with news wherever you are but also allow you to share, contribute to the news, decide on the quality of a news item by voting and commenting on articles and news items.

Wikis on the other hand are tools that allow you to add articles, information and data and edit existing ones to make them current.

Then there are the social-network sites which we will be focusing on in this book. They are the tools that allow you to become very sociable by making friends worldwide. This one-step medium will help you to create, build and get profitably branded through chatting, commenting on issues and profiles, joining groups and having discussions without having to use a separate medium for each activity.

To narrow down the focus, we will concentrate on social media sites like *facebook*, *LinkedIn*, *Twitter*, *Flikr* and *YouTube* and (just before publishing this book) *Google+* which allow you the professional to make friends, comment on profiles, join groups, attend activities online, have discussions that are of interest to you and your career. They will also enable you to share videos and pictures in a more professional manner as you pursue your goals on any social networking platform.

Chapter 2

WHAT EXACTLY IS
SOCIAL NETWORKING?

"All know the way; few actually walk it."—Bodhidharma

Gone are the days when manna fell directly from heaven. Manna is now wrapped in unexpected packages and if you want something, you have to take the initiative to attain it. That is why it is so important to connect with other people in order to search for and attain your goal that much easier. This is a skill every human being, especially business owners and professionals, must learn to accelerate the success process. Ironically, it is a skill that many lack, are not aware of, or ignore. Luckily, social networking sites have been created to make the building of mutually beneficial relationships very possible and global.

To explain what social networking sites are all about, one can say that they are our virtual world in real-time action!

As in the real world, it is existentially important to find people who you believe can compliment your efforts, associate with you and hopefully become good friends when you enter a new territory. Some become acquaintances, ordinary friends and very good friends, soul mates or trustees. Through the interaction, you may even realize there are potential people you can partner with to build your dream business, etc. However, it is quite likely that you may not have the opportunity to meet everyone in that community or perhaps you simply do not want to associate with particular people for your own personal reasons. This applies to social networks too. They are sites that allow you to make friends. As time goes on and you gradually get to know your friends better, you can determine in which direction to take the friendship.

As a professional or entrepreneur, I assume that your intention for joining these social networks is to find friends that can help you to build mutually beneficial relationships for the growth of your businesses. It does not mean that you must not make ordinary friends too but your main focus (I assume) is the growth of your business.

When it comes to building business and social networking, many business owners believe they can do whatever they like. Their decisions though, either attract the right people or ruin their efforts all together.

To benefit from these platforms as a professional or entrepreneur, it is important to constantly provide value for your friends and followers. This value does not only mean the free special report you send them or the free tele-seminars you hold (just to mention a few of the tactics used). It is mainly about how you treat them individually as human beings and friends within the relationship you enjoy, the respect you accord them and the constant selflessness and willingness to help. Actually, these are the types of values you must give in any relationship and—for that matter—on any social networking site if you are determined to prosper. Forget about the selling!

My very good friend Terry Brock has effectively redefined connecting in networking: ". . . connecting begins by determining the needs of other people and working on ways to help them achieve their own goals. By helping others, you are going to help yourself. It is the law of reciprocity in action."

These social networking sites are goldmines for small business professionals and, as such, it really is up to you to know how to go about them in order to meet the right friends who will help you to get profitably branded and grow your business while you help them achieve their goals too.

Remember, building healthy relationships is not a one-way affair. Both sides must contribute if it is to become mutually beneficial. There are times I have been become very involved with certain friends on certain social networking sites and even in real life, only later to feel used by them whilst I thought I was developing mutually beneficial friendships. From what I hear, I am not alone. Some people, especially on the social networking sites, simply do not understand reciprocity. They keep on making and losing friends because of the way they do things that offend others.

As a business owner or professional, you want to avoid a negative reputation and take a very unique approach to give you an edge over your competitors, and to become an exceptional and magnetic marketer. By the way, if you have worked hard to reach where you are in your career or business and want to take your expertise to the next level—or just someone who wants to get profitably branded in both your business and personal life—go to http://www.ohyoubehave.com/bookgift.html and claim the gift I have reserved for you that teaches you how you can positively impact more lives and be rewarded for your expertise so you can enjoy your preferred lifestyle.

As I said earlier, no human being is an island on their own. It is in your own interest, therefore, to look for the right quality of friends with whom you can nurture mutually beneficial relationships. Note the word "friends" because no one friend has the answers to all your questions. It is not all about a multitude of friends but "the right quality of friends" with the right character and attitude. Very importantly, a quality relationship is based on respect, good manners and etiquette—qualities that are so vital for fueling a healthy relationship.

That is what really matters most in life and on any social networking site. You are not just adding names to your friends' list but dealing with real people in real time who want to be given some level of respect, acknowledgment and recognition for what they bring to the friendship.

Chapter 3

BRIDGE OVER
TROUBLED WATERS!

The fast pace of the world today has generally turned us into a society with little respect both for ourselves and others. Some people care very little about others, but it is a fact of nature that the "Golden rule" still applies anywhere we find ourselves.

There are all sorts of energies flowing around. If only we allow ourselves the chance to go with the right flow, we will realize that the positive energies we are consciously or unconsciously avoiding have a much greater power over the negative energies that seem to be having the upper hand in the lives of some people.

A video of a presentation by Dr Sue Morter at a TEDxNASA event reveals that positive energies are two and a half times stronger than negative energies. We may thus conclude that the more we fight the forms of energies that surround us, the more friction we get!

I believe that is why some people encounter so many disasters. They are causing their negative energies (beliefs) to conflict with the natural positive energies that can allow them to grow happily and be fulfilled. In my opinion, this has resulted in the lack of peace in these people and certain nations, the divorce rates skyrocketing, wars, you name it.

With regard to social networking, these negative energies have resulted in all forms of distress, mistrust, misunderstanding, suspicion and bad feelings surrounding people. This is simply because they are not even showing respect to the laws of nature. If only these people will allow these energy forms to help them fulfill their tasks, they would reach their full potential, make the right friends with respect to social networking and attract the kind of projects they need to be successful in their professional careers.

Human nature is naturally prone to making sense of everything around us. For that reason, people will always try to draw some form of conclusion about any situation they find themselves in or about people they meet. It is your entitlement. You have the free will to do so and in fact, you must do so as often as is necessary.

On the social networking platform, it is therefore your duty especially, as a professional who wants to maintain credibility, to intentionally make your friends draw the right conclusion about you in order to get profitably branded. Do not send mixed signals and messages that cause your friends and potential friends to misjudge you. When that happens, you activate more negative energy and end up creating bad relationships that hurt either you and/or other people. Again, as Dr Morter stated in her video, the heart is the source from which most people make decisions. It is the bio-electric powerhouse in the body. According to her, the heart is 40 to 60 times more powerful than the brain. As a result most people will not make decisions based on their logical reasoning—although many think they do—but rather based on their emotions.

If the signals you send out are in complete resonance with what they feel, you are more likely to win them emotionally and build a mutually beneficial relationship. However, you risk blocking meaningful relationships if the opposite is the case. Don't even think you can force somebody to adjust to your ways. Everyone out there believes to some extent that they have the power and the right to do whatever they want, just like you do.

They are right because, according to Dr Caroline Leaf in her book "Who Switched Off My Brain?" everyone has his or her own combination of intelligence hence our unique way of thinking. Despite this uniqueness, we must as individuals learn to think and do things in a way that does not offend or hurt other people.

Kenneth Blanchard PhD wrote in a foreword to Dr Spencer Johnson's "Who moved my cheese?"—a great book on how to deal with change—that "Everyone knows that not all change is good or even necessary. But in a world that is constantly changing, it is to our advantage to learn how to adapt and enjoy something better."

As a professional you should not look at the social networking sites as just new platforms and tools to build a following and then go ahead with the bad old behavior of bombarding them with your products and services. To put more emphasis on this truth research indicates that mere technological control of a digital environment does not ensure educated use. There is need for an educational system that strongly emphasizes the development of creative and critical thinking skills among people exposed to digital environments.

What you must therefore be aiming for is to build mutually beneficial relationships that will benefit you for a very long time to come in a creative, caring and well-mannered way that is conversant with modern times. This involves being open to new ways of doing things with commitment.

Anthony Robbins' book "Unlimited Power" gives advice to that effect: "Know your outcome, model what works, take action, develop the sensory to know what you're getting, and keep refining it until you get what you want." It is not just enough to have all the strategic social media tools that will enable you to maximize your presence on the web. Nor is it enough to make friends and hope and pray that they will one day buy your products or services.

What matters is how committed, caring, selfless and honest you are in building mutually beneficial relationships based on integrity that last a long time, if not a lifetime. This includes learning to show respect and consideration to others who do things differently from what you are used to. It certinly means knowing how to do things right in this age of digital technology that is expanding and rapidly undergoing diverse changes.

Research conducted between 2004 and 2009 by Eshet-Alkalai & Amichai-Hamburger (2004) with the title "You Can Teach Old Dogs New Tricks" that investigated digital literacy skills among different age-groups revealed two major patterns of change over time. Further research by Eshet-Alkalai and Chajut (2009) that investigated changes over time in these digital literacy skills among the same participants five years later came to the same conclusion.

(1) closing the gap between younger and older participants in tasks that emphasize experience and technical control (photo-visual and branching tasks);

(2) widening the gap between younger and older participants in tasks that emphasize creativity and critical thinking (reproduction and information tasks).

Based on the results from the control groups, the researchers suggested that experience with technology and not age-dependent cognitive development accounts for the observed life-long changes in digital literacy skills.

What is most interesting in these research findings for the social media and social networking professional is the fact that the sharp decrease in information skills suggests that the ability to find information or use digital environments does not guarantee an educated or smart use of digital environments. Having been kindly given the privilege and permission to use the report, I believe it is vital to share some excerpts from the findings. It will give you a deeper understanding of how digital literacy functions.

As a professional social networking individual, it might interest you to know that in as much as you might think that you just need friends and the right digital tools to promote your products and services, there is more to it than meets the eye. You are digitally branding yourself in the process! These valuable research findings noted that the proliferation of digital technologies during the digital era confronts individuals with situations that require the utilization of an ever-growing assortment of technical, cognitive, emotional, and sociological skills that are critical for effective performance.

Despite its extensive use in the literature of findings, digital literacy has only a few theoretical models and the lack of sufficient empirical studies limits the researcher's knowledge about its utilization among specific gender, age, or social groups. However, a comprehensive conceptual model of digital literacy has been published. It comprises six literacy skills encompassing all the cognitive challenges faced by users of present-day digital environments as follows:

- **Photo-visual literacy skill:** Modern graphic-based digital environments require scholars to employ cognitive skills of "using vision to think" (Tuft, 1990) in order to create photo-visual communication with the environment. This unique form of digital thinking skill helps users to intuitively "read" and understand instructions and messages that are presented in a visual-graphical form, as in user-interfaces and in children's computer games (Shneiderman, 1998).
- **Reproduction literacy skill:** Modern digital technologies provide users with opportunities to create visual art and written works by reproducing and manipulating text, visuals, and audio pieces. This requires the utilization of a digital reproduction thinking skill, defined as the ability to create new meanings or new interpretations by combining pre-existing independent shreds of digital information as text, graphics and sound (Benjamin, 1994).
- **Branching literacy skill:** In hypermedia environments, users navigate in a branching, non-linear way through knowledge domains. This form of navigation confronts them with problems that involve the need to construct knowledge from independent sources of information that were accessed in a non-orderly and non-linear way (Spiro, Feltovitch, Jacobson, & Coulson, 1991). The terms "branching", "lateral" or "hypermedia thinking" are used interchangeably to describe the cognitive skills employed by users of such digital environments.
- **Information literacy skill:** Today, with the exponential growth in available information, consumers' ability to assess information by sorting out subjective, biased, or even false information has become a key issue in training people to become smart information consumers (Eshet-Alkalai & Geri, 2007, 2009). The

ability of information consumers to make educated assessments of information requires the utilization of a special kind of digital thinking skill, termed "information skill" (Bruce, 2003).

- **Socio-emotional literacy skill:** Users of collaborative digital environments, such as knowledge communities, discussion groups, and chat rooms are required to employ sociological and emotional skills in order to perform effectively in the mass communication of the cyberspace (Garrison, Anderson, & Archer, 2000). This new kind of digital thinking skill is termed "socio-emotional".

- **Real-time thinking skill:** Present-day multimedia environments, such as simulations and games, require that users process simultaneously large volumes of stimuli that "bombard" their cognition repeatedly. The ability of users to perform effectively in these environments is termed "real-time thinking" (Eshet-Alkalai, 2008a).

In as much as all of the above have something to do with you as a professional, what is very interesting especially in relation to social networking are the information literacy, socio-emotional literacy and real-time thinking skills. These are the immediate skills that, when well mastered, can help you to build the proper reputation, gain expert status and to be ever present in the minds of your target market to become the known, liked and trusted professional who is certainly the go-to person when it comes to issues pertaining to your field of expertise. In fact with this knowledge in your essential tools bag, you are on your way to getting profitably branded, something every professional must take into consideration in this day and age where there is so much confusion, frustration and lack of trust in the experiences people have today in our world economy.

To break it down a little bit more, you leverage your information literacy skill to provide your friends and digital audiences with valuable, worthy and useful information.

Your socio-emotional literacy skill helps you to communicate more effectively with respect and care to your friends because you send the right signals. This helps you to captivate their attention and to win points in their emotional bank account making it even easier for you to effortlessly convince them to invest in your expertise. Your real-time thinking skill, when well mastered, will help you offer advice, help and solutions to your friends in real time. Because they believe you must be the right person to provide relevant solutions, they will chat with you online or send you messages about their challenges—your way of comfortably converting them into paying clients or brand ambassadors who consistently put the word out about your expertise.

It is your duty as a professional to bridge that mystery gap between you and your potential clients and customers in order to reach their hearts. In fact, I see the social networking platforms as a bridge over troubled waters. The bridge is your way of dealing with others you make friends with on the social networking platforms and the waters are the relationships.

As already stated, there are so many troubled relationships around that hurt people. However, depending on the method used, we can use the social networking platforms to build a bridge over these troubled waters (relationships) and to create a better world.

My love for research made me find out more about bridges in order to better explain how this bridge concept works in our social networking activities. With the help of my civil engineer sister, here are some of the facts I discovered in relation to social networking.

Since we are dealing with troubled waters, the best bridge we need to build is a suspension bridge that is strong enough to hold for a long time. We otherwise risk collapsing and drowning!

What I learned is that a suspension bridge is held by cables. Because the bridge uses these cables as an integral part of the bridge design, it is flexible and affected by wind. Actually, engineers plan the design to take account of this and to increase stability!

When you think critically about this, you realize that you are the engineer of your social networking (suspension bridge over your relationships) success after all. Depending on how good or bad external (flexibility and wind influence) and human factors (both you and your friends' communication issues) affect you, you can either successfully build a strong bridge or one that the cables (social networking platforms) will not hold long for you.

Looking at our bridge again as engineers, we realize that it has superstructures and substructures. The superstructures above include the deck, towers and main suspension cables which to us professional social networkers represent our various social media and social networking platforms. These, just like any physical bridge, are those components that people see. However, there are those substructures below that include piers and anchorages without which a bridge is incomplete and unsafe. These are our beliefs, values and the relationships we build on these social networking platforms.

Without our beliefs and values, we are not unique individuals and without relationships, there can be no social networking or more importantly advancement in our lives.

With all these and other components of our individual idea of good-quality relationship, a design is necessary to build our individual bridge over these troubled waters. That will enable us to reach out in style to others across the world and to make real great friends to a level that is mutually beneficial to all sides regardless of how hard the "wind" blows. Engineering, designing and building your bridge depends therefore on the type of relationships you intend to have. This dictates which platforms are great for your particular situation; what impressions you want to create for yourself and to others; what style you want to use in your communications; what image and reputation you want to create and build; how you want to treat others and how you expect others to treat you; taking critical note of your beliefs and values as well as taking responsibility of the fact that all this can make or break you in your social networking activities. In a nutshell, how are you planning to design and build your brand?

It is all about crossing over to reach out to the other person, so it is your duty to design the right bridge that gets you there and is stable enough to hold for a lifetime.

You certainly do not want to build a functionally obsolete bridge because that would mean building a bridge that does not conform to the standards used today!

Such bridges are known to be inherently unsafe and will surely not be able to stand the pressures of the traffic and occasional floods. That is not the type you want to build as a professional. It's therefore advisable that you do some research and planning before you even continue with any social networking activity for business.

So . . .

Chapter 4

ARE YOU READY
TO GET ON BOARD?

"To create something exceptional, your mindset must be relentlessly focused on the smallest detail."—Georgio Armani

As a human being and especially as a professional, it is very tempting to be attracted by the bright shiny objects around you. You will agree with me that it can be very easy to jump onto a new idea that promises to help you advance in your career or business especially if you are someone who is very open to new ways of doing things. Much as it is good to be open to new ideas, it can also be very counter-effective if you do not put enough thought into it to find out how well it benefits you.

The essence is to use that idea to advance your personal development, your career or business without tarnishing your beliefs and values, image and reputation. Obviously, I am assuming that you have unraveled your purpose for wanting to join any social networking platform. It is very advisable to find out more about all those little bits of detail when joining any social network in order not to have regret afterwards.

Now, before dwelling on exactly what this means to your social networking efforts, there is something important to note: whatever you do as a professional, it is always best to decide on what philosophical position to adopt even before your first move. This might sound trivial and irrelevant, yet these are the fine details that help you to have the right foundation to start any social networking for professional reasons in particular. The reason is that it helps you to have control of the venture and to stay on course, have focus and to achieve the desired results.

On the other hand, without any philosophical stand, it is very easy to be swayed. This makes it almost impossible to achieve the desired results because you become susceptible to settling for anything except what you set out for originally. Not to mention the confusing messages you end up sending. That is why it is very important when you decide to become a part of any social networking platform, that you clearly know what you stand for, your values, and what you want to be known for. That helps you create the right image and reputation for yourself, your career or business thereby emerging profitably branded.

I remember when my business coach encouraged me to start social networking. I really did not have any idea how it would work for my business but since it looked promising for the long term, I decided to get on board and work my way patiently up to the point when I figure out how it could be of benefit.

I therefore decided to maintain my authentic and patient mindset, to start with, in order for me to position myself well as someone who advocates an achiever's mindset, passion, love and respect in any aspect of life. I made it a point to let my friends know exactly what I stand for and the kind of person I am in all activities that I undertake on the social networks I belong to in order not to fall victim to anything else that does not fit my beliefs and values or that can negatively affect my image and reputation.

A case in point was when a married woman I know very well invited me to join her in a dating social network in spite of the fact that she knows I have a husband to whom I am very happily married. I felt grieved by that, but I was patient and tolerant enough to explain to her why I would not join her on that platform. She stopped sending me messages and I guess my silence in the beginning made her assume I was thinking about it or had forgotten to join.

As a professional, in order to put across the right messages that tell people about your beliefs and values as well as strengthen your image and reputation, you need to have the right mindset.

You will have realized by now that interactivity on the internet these days is rapidly developing with so many tools and ways to communicate. The challenge really lies in your ability to tap into the right tools with the right mindset, to convey the right messages and emotions that affect you and your friends in a progressive, productive and positive way.

The first mindset to start with therefore is PATIENCE.

One disappointing message I have for you as a person joining a social networking site for career purposes is that it does not all happen overnight!

Just like building relationships in real life, you need to work on it and have the patience to gradually build the right relationships that will be beneficial to both parties in the long run. It really is all about looking at the long-term benefits and working gradually on that instead of jumping straight in and promoting yourself and your business and having too many expectations about how the platform can magically change your life in a jiffy.

That can seriously have adverse emotional effects on you as a person and on your credibility because of the disappointment. Also, with a patient mindset, you are able to control yourself and properly handle issues with your friends that you may encounter along the way. We are all liable to make mistakes but if you are impatient, you hurt yourself most of the time by taking issues personally with your friends.

Without a patient mindset, the worst thing that could happen is losing your credibility, thus losing the benefits of long term relationships that would benefit you in your career or business.

The second mindset you must assume when joining a social networking site is the COMMUNICATION mindset.

As a member of any social networking site, you must be conditioned to share information freely and be open-minded when communicating online because you will be dealing with all sorts of people from all walks of life. It is only your ability and skill to communicate correctly and clearly and express yourself in the right way that makes the other person truly get the message you want to convey, thereby either maintaining or improving your credibility and building the appropriate brand.

If you are the type of person who does not speak their mind and prefers one-way communication, then it is about time you shifted to the more engaging two-way communication—the ONLY way of communication that works on any social networking platform. As a professional or business person, it is very advantageous if you have the ability and skills to influence people.

Through good communication with your social networking friends and just desiring to build a mutually beneficial long term relationship with them, you can discover a lot about and from them that can enable you to inspire trust, build very strong relationships and open a whole new world of opportunities and benefits for you. However, you must know exactly how best to communicate in order to trigger the right emotions in them that will make you irresistible to them.

That means that you want to have a RELATIONSHIP BUILDING mindset because it is not all about the technology and the tools and strategies. It is basically about meeting real people in a professional and yet social way that allows you to build relationships with them in order to advance in your career or business in the long run. More often than not, many professionals believe that social media and social networking sites are all about the technology behind it, forgetting that the whole idea behind these platforms is to open the doors for individuals to build better relationships, for personal and professional reasons. This will be looked at in detail in another chapter.

Essential to note here is that it is a big mistake to assume the email marketing mindset in your social networking efforts. This entails just gathering email addresses and blasting their owners with sales promotion messages in their in-boxes. There is a word for that—SPAM! That certainly does not speak well of you as a professional, especially when you add their email addresses to your list without their permission.

In social networking, it is not about gathering names in order to send the link to your products, but rather building relationships that will in the long run benefit your business or career in varied ways. Looking at it exclusively from a sales point of view is very narrow, naïve and mediocre.

That is why you also need to have the AUTHENTICITY mindset that will help you build trust, credibility and create the right image for yourself and your business thereby getting profitably branded.

Unless you are authentic and people know you for who you are, you are only putting up a front which will eventually be discovered by your friends. This normally damages the relationship you are gradually building. Being honest and true to yourself is the only way to show that you are authentic and can be trusted. Unfortunately, some people rather capitalize on that authentic part of themselves that negatively affects their relationships.

It does not mean that because you want to be authentic, you must show how snobbish or rude you can be to people you think are not fit to be your friends. To be authentic, you must be open-minded enough to allow yourself to be open to your friends with a touch of politeness and some aura of class.

Note that just like the relationship mindset, the authenticity mindset also requires injecting a human touch of your professional self into the relationship-building process.

After all, you are not dealing with robots but real human beings. Therefore, consider how best you can build trust in them to boost your credibility by for example, making recommendations, commenting on what they discuss, referring them to other people and opportunities, to mention but a few examples.

This takes us to the next mindset you must have and that is CONTRIBUTION!

In social networking, especially for professional reasons, it is very important and strategic to contribute a lot in the forums and among your friends. Now, that does not mean barging in whenever there is a conversation just to be heard but rather contributing meaningfully and memorably. This does not mean giving away all your knowledge for free but you can still give advice, ideas and help without giving away the vault. There is one sure thing in social networking; you must be willing to give it your time.

Some of the ways to do this may be through recommendations, acknowledgments and connecting people together who you believe have things in common and can develop a good relationship.

So all in all, you want to present yourself more effectively and confidently as the preferred friend of choice. Simply put, become irresistible to the right potential friends who can help you take your career or business to the next level!

There certainly has been a lot of talk about credibility and being a leader in industry as a professional. That does not stop there, it even extends to people making friends on the social networking sites. Just on facebook alone, there are over half a billion people making friends. Just as there are those who do not mind who they make friends with, as a professional who wants to leverage the social networking sites for your business advantage, you must take into consideration with whom you make friends on any social networking site. What is meant is—Have a plan!

First of all, how do you effectively portray yourself as an authority and trusted professional to your prospective friends in order to print an indelible memory in their minds for them to want to be friends with you?

It is certainly not all about having just a large following on any social network or contributing halfheartedly or creating a great product. In the end, if you are found not to be competent, your followers will slowly but surely leave you.

It is vital to pay attention to whether you come across to your prospective friends as a person of authority and a confident expert in your field, yet kind, warm and someone worth making friends with.

One last mindset to mention here is the mindset of a COMMITED and CONSISTENT professional.

As stated earlier, you must have a plan for what you do in your career or business.

It doesn't have to be complicated or a full book to start with. It can just be a written one-page plan that outlines in brief what you intend to use the social networks for and how you will go about it to reach that goal.

Without a plan, you will begin to believe that social networking is a waste of time.

If you have some kind of a plan, take the time to research, know and join the social networks that can benefit you and your career and put together a feasible schedule, you are more likely to be committed and consistent with your social networking efforts because you will know you are making the right friends and you are clear about your purpose. That gradually helps you to develop the passion and desire to be more effective.

Remember, social networking is all about long-term gains and if you lack the right mindset to start with before you jump into it, it will become extremely difficult to achieve any meaningful results.

In order therefore not to fall behind and assume that social networking is a waste of time for your career, make a conscious effort to work on your social media and networking mindset and you will be amazed by the usefulness and cost effectiveness of it all. What this means to you is that you must be congruent, consistent, have the confidence and uniformity that portrays the authority and strong image you put out there. In effect, always appear to your social networking friends the way they believe an expert in your field must appear. Otherwise, you are asking them to look elsewhere for solutions. Remember that people DO make decisions based on emotions and the experiences they enjoy.

The heights you can take your business to in any medium, including social networking sites, with the confidence, appropriate professional mindset and etiquette to portray yourself as the first brand and friend of choice knows no limits. You will also have the confidence and ability to create the right environment that only attracts people who are ready and willing to bring you into contact with quality prospective partners and clients who will willingly engage your services or invest in your products.

One way to set the ball rolling is for you to start letting your integrity shine in any message you put out to your friends. Let them know that you are trustworthy!

It is important to note here that these messages need not necessarily only be in words but also, very critically, your actions which include how you approach people you want to make friends with, the quality of the videos you upload as well as the images you post, links and information you share and a lot more. As an individual, you must have noticed that you always want to have a sense of belonging. This means that you must behave in a specific way in order for other people to trust you or for them to feel comfortable with you being accepted in any community. Also, human as we are, we always demand that we are shown some level of respect, recognition and acknowledgment—no matter our level of education, standard of living, situation or circumstances in life. And these are very basic and true!

Unfortunately, there seems to be some kind of confusion, particularly on-line. Some professionals hide in front of their computers and assume that with the click of a button or mouse, their wishes must be fulfilled. It is sad to say that there is no Aladdin on-line! In as much as it is good to work smartly, working hard at building those relationships to make them meaningful and worthwhile is needed as well. These unfortunate professionals do not realize (or tend to forget) that those people they are sending messages to have emotions, feelings and a sense of responsibility (well, most of the time) and would not want to be "spammed" or tricked into doing anything against their will.

People need to wake up to the fact that doing things selfishly, without respect and consideration of others NEVER improves their chances of success. It does not matter whether it is on-line or off-line. That is why it is so necessary to learn some social networking etiquette skills if you are a member of any social networking platform. You see, social networking etiquette enables you to have the right mindset and to attract the right friends who are willing to help you forge a successful career or business.

Note, however, that much as social networking platforms can help you promote your career, business and your personal brand, it is not a quick-fix solution to your business or career challenges at all. It is the kind of relationships you nurture and the trust that exists in the relationships you have with people you are connected to that really matters.

Although this might be common wisdom, it is necessary to repeat that any relationship without trust will suffer greatly. So without much ado, let's dig right into the etiquette of social networking.

Chapter 5

WHY DO YOU NEED PROPER ETIQUETTE IN SOCIAL NETWORKING?

As Jeffrey Gitomer said, "Add the word 'grandma' silently to the end of each sentence. This reminds people that they shouldn't say things to customers that they cannot say to their grandma!"

Mr. Gitomer is very right. Some people today do not care what they say—not even to their great grandmas—and that is where good manners and proper etiquette come in handy, especially when one happens to be a professional seeking to advance one's career.

Interestingly, the Oxford dictionary describes the word "manners" as "polite or well-bred social behavior, social behavior or habits" and the word "etiquette" as "the customary code of polite behavior in a society." For that simple reason, since any social networking platform is a form of society, there must be certain customary codes of polite behavior that you especially as a professional must adhere to, although they may not be clearly spelled out in the rules and regulations of those social networking sites you belong to.

Much as it is good to know your table manners when you are a professional in business, your ability to make people feel comfortable in your company is even more important for them to want to do even more business with you.

Emily Post summed it all up in a quote: "Manners are made up of trivialities of deportment which can be easily learned if one does not happen to know them; manner is personality—the outward manifestation of one's innate character and attitude toward life . . . Etiquette must, if it is to be of more than trifling use, include ethics as well as manners. Certainly what one is, is of far greater importance than what one appears to be."

This is especially so on social networking platforms, where people often attempt to appear to be who they truly are not! Etiquette without thoughtfulness and kindness for others does not work and that is where manners play a role. What is important to know as a professional using social networking for business purposes is to treat others the way they want to be treated or the way you want to be treated yourself. Check your attitude and know that it is important to learn and practice those unspoken rules of etiquette for any social networking site you join and NEVER forget that the "Golden rule" works there too.

At this moment, I will digress a little and ask you to take a look at how people used to live years ago. You will realize that life in the past was more calm and, very importantly, there was at least one parent dedicated to bringing up the children. A lot of discipline was instilled in the children, teaching them how to respect themselves and others, take responsibility and become reliable people.

Today, the world is moving fast, economies are getting worse each day and in most cases, both parents MUST work in order to cater for the family. This has caused many children, through no fault of theirs, to grow up learning to care for themselves without gradual initiation into the adult world. The children are really not to blame. Apart from being forced to "grow up", they have been also forced to become what I call "Selfish Hero Conscious" and "self-esteem fanatics."

This simply means that many people are no longer humble, but rather more occupied with selfish aggrandizement, worldliness and extremely demanding instead of being value and principle conscious. This has caused many to adopt a selfish 'it's my right' and an irresponsible mindset which, unknowingly to them, is negatively affecting their outcomes because other people cannot trust or rely on them, let alone want to be near them.

All this, coupled with the advancement in technology which—if used properly and wisely is a blessing but seems to promise more than human beings can achieve in record time—has affected many people's behavior, making them less concerned about the ramifications of their actions and making human integrity in today's world look somewhat insignificant.

All these negative attitudes that are ingrained in many individuals are unfortunately very evident in the business world. Interestingly, no matter how much they try to act the "better person," the curtain eventually draws back and their true self is revealed. Nonetheless, there certainly are millions out there who value integrity.

I listened to Mr. Zig Ziglar's CD on the "Essential Strategies For Success" and found some of the research findings he mentions very revealing and essential. I would like to share them with you. According to Mr. Ziglar, "90% of all of the visits to medical doctors roughly is because of stress in their lives and nearly a 100% of all of our counseling comes because of relationship difficulties."

Mr. Ziglar's advice is that "if we can solve the stress problem by bringing it down a manageable size and learn how to get along with everybody, then we can make a huge impact on our career. We can focus on what we do best and what we love to do."

This just proves that your relationships with the people around you are very important no matter what aspect of your life it relates to, be it personal, business, career, online or offline. Practically speaking, there need not necessarily be any great difference between on-line and off-line relationships and behavior. However, technology has a tricky way of negatively influencing people's behavior if they are not very careful.

This means that you ought not to get too fascinated by the possibilities of today's technology and thereby forget the human beings with whose help you can realize your goals by using the technology available. You need to recognize, accept people and show respect to them on-line just as is expected of you in real situations off-line. Be nice and willing to help build mutually beneficial relationships with those you meet online. Avoid being nasty or selfish!

Note that as a professional, your goal must be to project and reinforce your brand, credibility and expertise in every action you take. You will never know who is following you or which of your friends is watching you and just finally getting convinced that you are the perfect choice for a project that could take your career to the next level. So it is up to you to determine if your actions are making you draw nearer to your aim and success or failure. Always keep at the back of your mind that what people think about you is what they believe is true in regard to your actions, especially online where they cannot see you physically to determine who you really are!

For emphasis on etiquette in business once again, professionals should not collect the email addresses of their social networking friends and put them on their business mailing list without permission. It certainly does not speak well of you, your professional brand and your integrity at all!

We now have social networking sites that have created the avenue and opportunity for people to be free to connect in a global village, express themselves, share information and maximize their potential. As a professional, you must pay particular attention to your online behavior. Depending on how focused you are, your behavioral patterns in these media can greatly increase or reduce your success. No matter how wonderful you personally think you are or how great your product or service may be, think first of how you can build an impeccable reputation and brand image. Avoid using marketing strategies that promise to increase the sale of your products or services, without considering the negative implications attached to them in the long run.

There certainly are very good marketing strategies out there that you can use to flood your business with customers and clients but no matter how good the strategy may be, if you do not have a good umbrella brand strategy that enables you to enhance your reputation and image, you will be the loser in the long run. A fine professional with good manners and etiquette gets his or her competitive edge over the herd on any social networking site by giving the right impression to their friends and online followers and thereby attracting the people they target.

Surprisingly in socializing, it is the little things that make you exceptional from the herd. You definitely will become exceptional with the appropriate impression to attract the necessary attention you need for yourself and your business. An example is to show respect both to yourself and your friends on any social networking platform you join—the basis of etiquette. That is what people respond to best to enable them build trust in a person or a brand. As you seek or leverage any social networking site for your career purposes, you have to recognize that your credibility in regard to your friends and clients depends on you giving them their due respect in line with what they expect of you in a social setting. People DO have expectations of how a particular person should behave in respect to his or her profession. So if you act otherwise, you end up tarnishing your brand image.

Secondly, do not forget to allow your friends, clients and potential clients to enjoy their personal space in any way you can make that possible. It is your way of showing them respect and allowing them to gradually start wanting to trust and know you better. People cherish their personal space. You can call it their territory. Anytime this personal territory seems to be invaded, from personal experience, you will agree with me that it becomes uncomfortable and you begin taking steps to protect your territory like moving away or avoiding the situation, depending on your personal attitude.

That is what happens on the social networking platforms too. People tend to avoid those who make them feel uncomfortable by (depending on cultural background) asking them too personal questions, posting certain things on their wall or pages without their permission and intruding in conversations that does not concern them. You get the drift I hope.

As you may have well understood by now, in order to be effective in your profession or career, you need to be able to know how to simply win people emotionally because their buying is mainly based on emotions.

Also, as human beings, we always want to feel a sense of belonging, appreciation and acknowledgment. Therefore you, as a professional, need to know the thoughts, feelings and emotions of the people you want to attract as friends and eventually do any business with. Know what they will and will not respond to favorably to in order to gain their attention.

People want to be treated as individuals and the more you are able to communicate that respect and attention individually, the easier it will be for you to succeed in your social networking activities and your business too. You will inevitably be making your friends feel special and as a result, they cannot help but draw closer to you and help you in any way they can.

Now, don't get limited in your thoughts because your ability to show respect to your friends and clients and target market does not mean just saying "please", "thank you" and "sorry" (although they are all equally important). It also extends to your own personal manners and comportment both offline and online. Put in another way, it is that extra 'personal humble touch' that you add to the friendship that will trigger the right emotions to make the relationship special.

In other words, do you personally take the conscious effort to show respect, care, particular attention and genuine love through all that you do and say?

An example of rudeness that just doesn't fit a professional or business owner in social networking, is to just click on the "add friend" button when you want to send an invitation to be friends with someone without adding a simple small message. Interestingly enough, many simply take it for granted. We shall get into more details about this habit later.

Simply showing respect to your friends does not only earn you their respect, but also their trust. Trust is most essential for any professional in today's business environment that is rampant with pretense and fraud. It is through people that you can build your business, so there is a great need for you to stand out from the crowd and glow with your genuine respect for them. This takes us to the next vital issue of proper social networking etiquette—communicating clearly!

It is so important to stress the fact that in order to be able to build trust among people and your target market, you need to be very clear in all your communication. Engaging in communication with your friends on any social networking platform is by far the simplest way to get to know them better and to build a trustworthy, long term relationship. Yet many times people put messages on their profiles or comments, or even send personal messages that leave you wondering what they mean. As a professional, you must never assume your friends understand what you want to communicate and the language in which you want to communicate to them. It will amaze you how people misunderstand simple words you may assume are common in a given language.

In order not to assume things or expect people to react in particular ways—which will disappoint you eventually if you do—YOU must rather let go of your assumptions and do your best to communicate in a manner that makes your communications as simple and comprehensible as possible. For that reason, always make your communication clear and straightforward in a way that will make it easy for your friends and followers to understand exactly what you are communicating to them.

The fact that many people these days use the internet in some form as their online communication channel does not mean that you, as a professional, should assume they MUST understand the language you use online. In fact it would be very naive to think and act in such a way in your capacity as a professional because people would then misunderstand you or have the wrong impression about you. For that matter, it is always best to avoid doing things your own way but rather take hints from how your friends communicate with you, the choice of words for instance, in order not to send out wrong signals.

When your communication continually tends to contain such wrong impressions and signals, you force the recipients to naturally ask themselves if you really know what you are talking about and if you are worth their friendship at all, let alone competent enough to engage in any meaningful relationship with them. That is why it is always wise to think about how to communicate clearly to develop long-lasting relationships with your social networking friends and any friendship for that matter, if you intend to reap some benefits.

These are the basics of etiquette—making people feel comfortable and respected in your company by sending out the right signals and messages! Believe it or not, people want to be treated as individuals and with some level of respect regardless of how much morals have sunk in the world today.

Not communicating right is consequently a recipe for disaster because you will be allowing others to brand you inappropriately—a bad strategy for business growth and success and certainly not the right way to get profitably branded.

Thanks to technology, meeting potential clients and building relationships is now much easier.

The influx of social media including social networking, forums, chat rooms, instant messaging and a whole lot more have provided individuals particularly professional business people and entrepreneurs the tools with which to maximize potential and profits and to take careers and business to the next level.

It is important to note that they are just tools! Yet that is what many professionals and entrepreneurs fail to recognize. Just like any physical tool, there are specific ways in which these social media tools can be properly used for maximum benefit and to get profitably branded.

I am not talking about just how to type in your name or upload your logo, picture, post updates when it comes to your profile page on a social networking site or the applications that will get you well connected and visible. I am talking about your ability as a professional to use these tools in the proper manner that makes you create an image and build the reputation that you desire for your long-term business goals.

Some marketers tell you that as long as you can type on a keyboard, you can start an internet business. Unfortunately, that is just a minute part of the whole truth. There is more to building a successful business than meets the eye. If you study real successful businesses and careers, you will for instance realize that it is the local handyman's attention to detail and concern for how the family is doing when he comes to fix the broken sink or dishwasher in the home that creates an impeccable impression. This qualifies him for a word-of-mouth recommendation.

You may also remember that the employee who superbly gets along with other co-workers and managers, in addition to his or her good work, quickly gets promotion or the opportunity to work on certain projects that other colleagues only dream of.

You are also more comfortable shopping in that particular local shop because you know where to find what you want to purchase, the people recognize you and smile back at you, ready to help you find that particular product you seem unable to locate on the shelves.

That is not forgetting the helpful lady at the till and her enthusiastic good wishes till the next time you come shopping again.

Similarly in the virtual world, you will agree that it just feels good to surf and find a professionally built website that gives you the information you want and more. These days it even goes further to give you the opportunity to interact on the page you have landed on and if possible share the information you have found with friends you believe could benefit from it. This makes you gradually build some trust in the person or people behind the website you are visiting and you can't help consequently wanting to build a better relationship with them which you believe is secure, safe and reliable.

Relating to social networking is a very strong phenomenon in the digital world today. If you are able to communicate clearly with your friends and followers, they tend to be attracted to you and genuinely have respect for you. Since under normal circumstances you are eager to make friends with those who act professionally and mature in their activities both offline and online, the same phenomenon will apply on the social networking sites. You will consequently attract the appropriate kind of people on those social networking platforms you belong to, depending on your way of doing things.

Also very importantly, since we now deal with a multicultural world, paying attention to your intercultural communication in both your social and business interactions online can take your business to the next level on any social networking site you decide to join. It is a multicultural virtual world where people expect you to acknowledge and show respect to their beliefs and values too! So the faster and better you are able to master these and other powerful skills, the faster it will be for you to reap the rewards that come with them.

Interestingly, it can be very easy to make your multicultural friends feel comfortable thereby reaping many benefits. However, many individuals and professionals either just take this for granted or ignorantly keep on creating stereotypes. Overall, it has become one of the strategic aspects that most professionals and entrepreneurs overlook to their business peril.

It is of advantage and benefit to professionals if they can transform themselves into persons who use the right and proper etiquette in their business and social networking to address those friends from diverse cultures.

Showing respect and recognition helps to maximize the probability of long-term relationships. This makes it easier to build trust and credibility, while subsequently maintaining and even increasing sales because such actions inevitably makes you emerge profitably branded. The customers always see you as their only preferred choice, which is the place you want to be to reap repeated benefits by making friends with people of diverse cultures and to ultimately bring your expertise to the international market.

One other thing to be aware of is that human beings are very resistant to change.

What that means to you as a professional is that the more your friends feel comfortable with you, the more they will be willing to spend more time finding out how you can help them and vice versa. As they gradually feel comfortable with you, they will also drop their defenses and objections to spending their hard-earned money on your products.

This is because they tend to believe and know that they can trust their friend (you) with their hard-earned money due to the level of respect and overall treatment you give them. They are happier and more relaxed giving their money to you and recommending you to other friends.

Consequently, this makes them feel more compelled to build a stronger, healthier and a long-term relationship that translates into more profits for your business.

One pearl of wisdom from W. Clement Stone is: "Be careful with the friends you choose, for you will be like them." For this reason, it is very crucial that you consciously make efforts to attract the right quality of friends. If you are familiar with the law of attraction, then you know that you attract what you focus on and that "birds of the same feather flock together." This is also very true of the kind of friends and potential clients you attract to your business through your social networking.

In this new era, where there are seemingly many ways to solve one particular problem, potential clients and customers are now becoming very selective of who they give their money to because they are very cautious when choosing the right solution for their situation.

You might think all that is needed to run a business is a strong marketing strategy and possibly a lot of friends on some social networking sites. The truth is that people are not paying too much attention to most of the marketing tricks these days because there is too much information out there. They are now being discreet and seeking information from friends they believe they can trust. After all, next to our feelings, is that not what we do in the real world—asking our most trusted friends for information?

More than ever before, clients and customers are seeking credible and authentic business owners with whom they believe their money will be well worth spending and will enjoy a memorable experience as a result of making that particular purchasing decision.

Your chances of surviving, let alone thriving in this particular economic condition, is now highly dependent on your unique personal "Brand of One" that people believe will give them that unforgettable experience depending on how you treat them as individuals.

This simply means that treating people the way they want to be treated is more likely to get them wanting your friendship for a longer time and, who knows, they might be the people to buy from you and recommend you to the right partners and clients because they tend to sell for you before you even get in touch with the "usual" customers.

Just in passing, it has been proven that it costs seven times more to find a new customer than to maintain one. That is one very potent reason why you strongly want to consider getting profitably branded as a professional and a small business owner.

So why would you want to keep hunting for new customers if it makes economic sense to treat your friends and existing clients with some respect and recognition? Giving them respect and recognition enables you to maintain them and to have them do the promoting of your products and services for you as long as you are working with a strategy that gets you profitably branded?

These are just a few ways proper and professional business etiquette, including general netiquette and social networking etiquette, can strongly help you build long-term relationships with your prospective friends and clients on the social networking sites so that you get noticed by the right people, attract quality clients and consequently get paid handsomely for your expertise.

Regardless of whether you do business online or offline, if you are able to master professional etiquette, you put an aura of class around your business and your persona that is obvious to potential clients whether you tell them or not. Believe it or not, people like it as long as it's not a bluff.

This is true for attracting quality friends and clients to boost your business in general. Not only do you convey and attract the right emotions, you also scale up your credibility and consequently get better results for your actions.

I will end by quoting Carl W. Buechner who said, "They may forget what you said, but they will never forget how you made them feel." And that is the mark of a profitably branded professional or small business owner.

Chapter 6

WHO ARE YOU AND
WHAT ARE YOU UP TO?

There is nothing more important to begin with than to be yourself as a professional joining a social networking site for business. John Jakes so well summed it up: "Be yourself. Above all, let who you are, what you believe, shine through every sentence you write, every piece you finish." How relevant—especially when we are dealing with a virtual world where nothing put out there is ever lost.

In relation to social networking sites, your profile page is the start to being yourself and creating the right impression among others! For that reason, let us look at how you can create the right impressions online and be yourself starting with your profile.

Creating a profile that gets you profitably branded by representing your business and you personally is one very important piece of social networking that you must never forget as a professional.

The Oxford dictionary defines a "profile" as "a short descriptive article about someone," and "the extent to which a person or an organization attracts public notice."

Particularly on the social networking sites, you always should give the right and appropriate description of yourself as a professional and create an enduring first impression. That is the basis on which people at that moment decide whether you are worthy of their company or not. It is all you have to show and tell people about yourself and why they ought to choose you as a friend over all those other professionals who provide services similar to yours and whose profile pages they have visited in their quest to make new friends.

In any situation you find yourself, such as meeting new people especially for business, your chances of getting a second chance is minimal. For that matter, you need to present your best possible self every time. It doesn't mean that you may not meet rejections. There are people you will encounter who may just not like you through no fault of yours. Creating the right impression however, gives you the confidence to present yourself to the best of your ability and reduces the likelihood of rejection.

The way you present yourself as an individual and a professional—from your body language through conversations to your clothing—says a lot about the amount of respect and self-confidence you have both for yourself and others.

That goes a long way to tell the prospective friend whether you are in control of yourself and your business and therefore whether it is safe to transact any business with you or not.

This is even more critical online because you really, in essence, have just your photograph as a first step to create that likeable factor to make a person continue reading your profile details. It is therefore important as a professional on a social networking site to be able to sell yourself positively right from the first time anybody lands on your profile page.

In fact just to give you some insight of a research finding by the BBC News, it has been found out that the attention span of the average human being since the emergence of the internet has reduced drastically to 9 seconds. So all you have as a professional is 9 seconds on any social networking site to make that lasting first impression.

Just stating that you are a professional on your profile page(s) is not enough to convince "visitors" because not only is it likely that they might not read it but anyone can type that on their profile with a picture showing a bare chest on the beach. You are entitled to do that as long as you are a professional surfer or a bay-watch. What truly proves you are a professional and a savvy business person is your appropriate professional picture that visitors immediately see when they come to your profile page, followed by your choice of words, presentation and online behavior.

It is your duty to make people like and be attracted to you in a way that makes them want to engage and be willing to talk business with you, pay for your services and see your brand as the only solution to their problem.

Experiments by psychologists have revealed that all it takes is a tenth of a second to form an impression of a stranger and naturally, people judge you by what they see and the impression they have of you in the very first few seconds of having an encounter with you. The interesting part of these facts is that over 80 percent of the impressions are based on nonverbal signs.

In other words, what you actually tell people has very little to do with how they judge and perceive you. That means that once you create a first impression, trying to change their mind is difficult!

This situation is even worse on any social networking platform on the internet where people spend only seconds on a particular page, including your profile page.

When you meet new people online who want to make friends with you, your chances of getting a second chance at them is minimal. For that reason, you need to present your best possible self at all times. That means that you need to have an excellent photograph that will attract them to read further. Use decent language at all times.

One online aspect that is quite similar to the offline world is that most people would rather not talk about anything that embarrasses them or comment on other people's bad behavior. They would rather let you be who you are. They either avoid you as much as they can or cease to be friends with you. So, much as you want to be yourself, you also want people to know that you respect them and, most importantly, yourself and that you are professional too.

That does not mean that you must be all uptight. It only means that as you present yourself appropriately to the public, let them know the true you and your professional side too. It is not just about being likeable but showing that you are a person of integrity, value and respect.

You certainly can talk about your personal life and that makes you very human and more approachable. However, avoid washing your dirty linen on the internet. Nobody is interested in that anyway. It only shows bad etiquette and manners which further damages your reputation and social networking relationships in the long run, consequently weakening your brand potency.

In as much as the word is "social", as a professional, you should exercise a great level of caution in order not to send the wrong messages at anytime whatsoever.

In general, your use of proper etiquette in this sense is what you use to show what words alone cannot tell. That is why it is very important to understand that a good profile photograph is so essential in social networking.

Like your product or service, you must present yourself very attractively and worthwhile. For example, your appearance as a lawyer must not be similar to that of the professional baseball coach.

You certainly may post whatever photograph you like. However, you should also note that you are representing both yourself and your business online and therefore the image you present must positively favor both. As a professional, just because you love mountain-climbing does not mean everyone will be interested in that picture on your profile page nor is everyone—apart from yourself—going to be attracted to whatever other image you upload. Rather save those pictures in your online photo-album.

Also, let the information you provide on your profile page or anywhere online be relevant to and reflect your professionalism as you deem appropriate. This means checking your choice of words, the impression you create and how you come across to others.

It is fairly acceptable if you decide to add some personal information to your online presence.

However, as mentioned and advised earlier, you must make the conscious effort to ensure that your online communications are all helping you put across the right image that enhances your professional brand.

Be aware that you are only reinforcing your personal brand online with any activity you undertake. Make sure this is exactly what you want to put across because people identify you with the kind of brand you create for yourself or, in the worst case, they will create one for you that you may not like. You don't want to provide information or create impressions that could be used against you and your business or your profession.

Here in Germany—and in many other countries too—there is a rapid emerging phenomenon of companies now searching people's profiles and activities online before employing them. As a professional who may be seeking employment, your prospective employer may have read all about you and your activities online even before you enter the interview room. That doesn't sound fair but it is the reality these days. And I am very sure it is the same with business people too looking to enter into business with certain particular companies and potential partners

As friendships develop with my online friends, they tell me they chose me as a friend all because of what I put online. Most of them are worlds apart from me.

Personally, I make people realize that I am a student of life. I enjoy living my preferred lifestyle with integrity and I take a no excuses approach when it comes to my reputation. These are the messages and signals in my pictures, videos and words that I put online.

It is said that a picture tells a thousand words. That is exactly what it does on your profile page on any social networking site you join. Personally, I can be a very serious person yet I make sure that I have my fun and enjoy life to the fullest. I am very relaxed as well and love enjoying the company of other people. This is what English describes as extrovert and that is exactly what my online image shows.

All of my profile pictures in the social media have a professional image that—from the comments I get—indicates my friends feel my authenticity.

There are two particular friends of mine whose profile pictures I like to look at so much because they give them a particular image that I am comfortable with. One of them gives me the impression that she is always happy and that nothing can put her off because she will just brush it aside and move on in her life. Guess what? She is a spirit coach and that certainly fits in her profession and social media presence.

The second friend is a celebrity on facebook and a business development strategist. His profile picture tells me exactly that! He did not go into a studio to take a "professional picture" but his picture projects professionalism at its best and he looks it straight away. He is a no-nonsense person. I see him as someone who will not tolerate any nonsense yet not snobbish. He is simply very professional and truly, getting to know him better day in and day out, it is exactly so. That is him, period! So be cautious about what image you present on any social media.

Being in a virtual world, just like in the real world, does not give you any excuse to create a false impression or hide who you are. In the long run, your real self will come out and you might hurt your reputation, your personal brand image and yourself.

My advice is therefore to try as much as possible to avoid uploading group or pet photographs, logos or any image on your profile page except your own personal picture. Remember that people are there to make friends with YOU and not your business or pet or any other image you present on your profile page. Reserve your logos for your business page or group(s) and the rest for your albums. They will fit perfectly there.

Once again for emphasis, it is just like being in the real world. Trying to always put up an image that is not you is counter-productive. Sooner than later, people will find you out and most often the results are not so pleasant.

Quoting Cheri Huber—and also attributed to my friend and mentor, T. Harv Eker: "How you do anything is how you do everything." That is why there is a need to use applications in moderation because they can clutter the profile page and give the impression that it is untidy, clumsy and unfocused. In my opinion, applications are some of the additions that liven up social networking communities. I see these applications as accessories from which to choose for your "WOW!"-effect and surely nobody wears all the accessories he or she owns when they go out.

Remember that although you are social networking, you are doing so in your capacity as a professional. Therefore you must 'dress up' professionally to create and give the right impression. For that reason, it does not reflect well on you professionally when you have every widget or application installed on your profile page. You may say you don't want to offend your friends when they send you the applications and widgets to be a part of their community.

Well, my question is, do you attend all the parties and other events your friends invite you to in real life situations? That would drain you totally, so why do that in the virtual world? I know it is just a click of some buttons but why do it just for the sake of doing it?

My answer as to whether you should accept all the applications sent to you by your friends is a big NO! The fact that your friends may send you the applications to join a particular game, cause or project does not mean you are obliged to do so. If that is part of why they joined the social networking site, fine! And if you also joined to be part of such a cause, then good for you too. If not, then please reflect on your original plan for joining the social networking site in the first place and think through to find out if the widget or application you are about to install is in alignment with your objectives and will enhance your personal image on your profile page.

This is very similar to some offline networking mistakes some professionals do. Some professionals complain that networking is a waste of time. What they fail to realize is that not all networking events are appropriate for them. So as long as they fail to plan and do some research on any networking event they intend to attend, networking will inevitably remain a waste of time for them and they will be missing out on a great strategy to first get profitably branded and second, grow their business.

So the next time you are about to upload an application, ask yourself whether it has any relevance to you as a person or your career. Remember, too much of everything is bad! Likewise, too many applications can actually slow down access to your profile page. This is frustrating and guarantees that the potential friend will just give up and look up someone else's profile that is easy to access. There goes your million-dollar business opportunity or your next opportunity to take your career to the next level!

Chapter 7

RESPECTING SPACE
AND PRIVACY

Respecting people and people's personal online space—especially on social media in general—is something that is still lacking when one observes the way some professionals behave!

As human beings, we all like to enjoy our personal space no matter what. In a way, it makes us feel we are in control of our own situations. Thus, we are more comfortable dealing with others in a nicer and somewhat confident manner.

So the fact that a social networking site allows you to be free to do what you want there or the fact that you become a friend of someone on any of the social networking sites does not give you the "license to bombard", sorry, I mean the right to do whatever you want with them.

Just as in the real world, people and groups online also have their personal space that they want to guard and keep as well as want to be treated with some degree of respect.

The ring tone that I believe you should have in your mind (if you do not have it already) is that social media is all about building relationships!

No other way will win you online friends, so please focus rather on building meaningful relationships that make people genuinely want to know, like and trust you by respecting their personal space. There is no need to crowd them or inundate them with links and information just for you to be in touch with them without carefully thinking through if it is worth the effort for both parties.

You may have the best life-changing product or service in the world but being pushy would rather make people doubt if you are credible and if they should believe what you are saying.

Learning to build relationships first and giving to the community by selflessly helping others in ways you are capable of is the only way to genuinely and truly put yourself on stage.

It is from there that they will start finding out about you themselves and those who need your services will contact you. Through that, you get recommendations through friends who talk about your products or services to others.

Truly, there is nothing stronger than the good old word-of-mouth promotion you do not have to pay for, but is willingly done for you by people who know you and believe in what you do. In addition, respect personal space in conversations. Do not keep sending messages when your friend has not yet responded to your previous message unless it is a point you forgot to mention to back up what you wrote. This is the equivalent of crowding your partner in a conversation, not allowing him or her to have a say and pointing fingers at him or her in a conversation in the physical sense of it.

Also, be careful of the language you use with your social networking friends. Using slang may be OK for your very close and personal friends. However, you should know that people naturally have the tendency to be sensitive and irritated about certain slang or the use of foul language in any form.

You might also like to talk to friends about other people. However, make sure that you are not always gossiping, complaining and demeaning others. First of all, it does not speak well of you and I'm afraid you will not get far with this behavior. Instead, see how best you can be a resource to offer productive and positive information to your friends.

Some people like to keep their private lives very private and out of their professional lives. This is social media but it does not oblige you to share your private life if you feel uncomfortable doing so. By all means, don't disclose anything that you do not want to make public. After all, you are an individual and you have the right to your privacy. The fact that these networks ask you for some information does not mean you need to make them public.

When I started social networking, I had no idea how the system works. I thought it was a MUST to add all those details. Yes, I admit I was that naive! I somehow felt uncomfortable giving out certain information, so I started deleting some of it after a few days to see what the sites would do. I soon realized that it did not affect my membership to the sites at all.

An example is disclosing your full date of birth which can lead to identity theft. The safe thing to do is to leave out your birth year and display only the day and month in which you were born if you wish to show your birthday at all. However, it does not mean that you must shut your social networking friends out of your world and share only your name and business-website address.

By all means, feel free to tell people about yourself because it helps them to know whether you are fit to become their friend or not. Remember that people are on these sites first to make friends with YOU and, after enough trust has been built, then probably do business with you.

Provide information that would not make people think that you are hiding something from the public eye. After all, those who genuinely want to know you will use other means to find out more about you if you do not make the information available. That is a fact!

Be careful not to assume that you may readily use contact details of your friends on their profile pages because they are available online. Always ask which medium of contact is the right one to use before communicating with your friends outside social networking. For all you know, the telephone is in the control of another person or the email address on the profile page is not used as often as you may expect. I know many social networking friends who have confirmed to me that they pay more attention to their social networking messages than those in their e-mail boxes.

Therefore you are more likely to get your friends to respond to your call or message when you send it through the medium recommended to you because you asked their permission first. That is a great way for them to expect your message outside the social networking platform.

Subsequently, never reveal confidential business information to friends on social networking sites. You might not find it harmful but you can never know how someone may use that information or in whose hands the information might land. It really is in your own interest to draw the line between private, confidential and publicly acceptable information.

Chapter 8

How To Search For People And The Etiquette Of Making Friends

As a professional, it is essential you do your homework well in order to put together a quality list of significant people you want to be friends with. It's no longer what you know but who you know and also, as my friend Mari Smith says, who knows you!

Plenty of opportunities exist for you as a professional to find new friends on social networking sites and in social media in general. The few I will mention here are friend finder on facebook or the master search button on top of your facebook page and twellow or exectweets on twitter. They all give you the opportunity to choose from various categories of friends. So assuming you have your eyes set on business executives, musicians, work-at-home moms or coaches, these are very useful tools you can leverage to find those sorts of friends.

Russell H. Conwell very nicely puts across a message in his book "Acres of Diamonds" that most of the time, you don't need to look too far from yourself. As such, I advise you not to immediately jump-start with these tools but to look out for the right quality of friends with whom you feel you already have something in common and from which a meaningful relationship can easily grow.

In this chapter, I will remind you of all those great avenues you can use to find good and targeted friends right in your back yard!

In a traditional sense and by definition, quoting the Oxford dictionary, "friend" means "a person with whom one has a bond of mutual affection . . ." and "a person who supports a particular cause or organization." So when we say someone is our friend, we mean a person with whom we have mutually understanding and a beneficial relationship, as it should be!

However, the meaning and definition of "friends" in social networking can sometimes be very interesting. In making friends, you can use proper etiquette in order to build mutually beneficial relationships that inspire trust in your friendships and yield the appropriate results you joined the community for. That is why you must not rush into making friends on any social networking site. In fact, you are not obliged in the first place to make friends with all those who send you a request or with all those you discover on the social networking sites just to make the numbers!

In the physical world, there are many quotes about friendship but one that resonates well with me is by W. Clement Stone: "Be careful with the friends you choose, for you will become like them." This is true for both the physical world as well as the virtual world.

Professionals must make sure they have clear minds about why they want to join any social networking site at all in the first place and what their overall goal is. Having a clear mind about these basic things will help you not to waste your time and resources. In fact, if you have a plan of action for joining any social networking site, you will realize that not only will you be making quality friends but also gradually building strong, mutually beneficial relationships hence creating a win-win environment all the time.

My principle is to make friends with people you would feel comfortable with and proud to be around in real life as well as people you would not feel shy introducing to others or worry they might embarrass you. These are the ideal friends you should focus on.

One of the basics of etiquette is to make people feel comfortable in your presence. In the same way, it is sensible and ideal for you to also feel comfortable in the other person's company because you then feel more relaxed and the interaction flows naturally, an important ingredient for any lasting relationship.

Many people, especially business owners, jump into social networking and social media without any definite plan but only want to make "friends" or have "followers" for the purpose of promoting their products and services.

However, in as much as you can use social networking and social media to promote your business, you must also note that good manners are as important in the virtual world as they are in real world business. This is because they not only help you create the right impression and image you need for your business, they also help you to set yourself apart from your competitors, show that you are civil, self-controlled and that you have respect for others as well as yourself. In other words, they make you an exceptional professional!

So it is best to first decide what you personally hope to achieve with your social networking venture. In this case, you should have some kind of guideline around which to work and know the general profile of people you believe it is possible to build a lasting and quality relationship with.

Luckily, the virtual world makes this very easy for you in the sense that if you do not know the person at all, or the person does not have the qualities you want in a friend, you can either do a Google search of their names to know more about them or just ignore the request.

However, if the person sending you the request is someone you already know but would rather not be connected with in any social networking site, then good etiquette demands you politely send them a brief message informing them you would rather prefer not to be connected with them online. Please give a short reason. That's it!

In the physical world, you do not make friends with every Tom, Dick and Harry so why do that online just because someone has sent you a friendship invitation?

If you stick to your values and principles and let them guide you in all you do, including making friends on any social networking site, you will not go wrong.

One of the keys to living happily and enjoying a successful life is building quality and meaningful relationships. This includes your immediate and extended family members, co-workers, business partners or friends that stick with you through thick and thin.

Nonetheless, making friends on the social networking sites and in social media can also get complicated, for example when making friends with your ex-husband, ex-wife or ex-friend.

Now, it may sound awkward but how do you make friends with your ex-friend who you wish would never come into your life again? But first, let's start with the family.

Family members: One school of thought believes that in a true relationship, there must necessarily be no secrets. Another believes that in order to have a healthy relationship, you must not tell your partner everything. Certainly, there is truth in both depending on who you are with and the kind of relationship you want to nurture.

For this reason it is even more necessary to know how to build better relationships, especially in social networking sites when it comes to family because you never know which family member may bring you into contact with a major business partner online.

It is not my place to teach you how to run your family but there is one thing I know for sure and that is, good etiquette at home helps the family to be much happier and get along very well.

Good etiquette at home helps to build strong character and self confidence with built-in courtesy. It creates a safe haven for all the family members and guides them to live up to expectation and to selflessly help one another while taking responsibility for their individual actions. This also applies to making friends with any family member on any social networking platform.

Just as in the real world, learn to respect the privacy of the other family member who is now an online "friend". It is absolutely bad manners to use the social networking medium for snooping or reading messages from their friends or finding out what kind of friends they have or their activities. Politeness must by all means be extended to your online communication with family members. Do not be intimidated if you are not allowed to see certain things online by a family member "friend". Simply respect their privacy! After all it is their personal space and you MUST respect that.

Also, in as much as you must be willing to share, consider the age and level of understanding of the family members you have as "friends" on the social networking sites. Assuming you are friends with your child, will you feel free to share the same jokes you share with your professional colleagues? I don't think so, and you surely will not want him or her to hear things that you discuss with your other adult friends.

When it comes to raising children and creating a peaceful and safe haven for all family members, it is always good to take every medium into consideration. By practicing good manners and etiquette in your family, it will help you to know if it is appropriate to make friends with a particular family member online or not.

Remember that as a parent and a professional, you are a full-time role model. Both your family members and business colleagues will reciprocate whatever action you take accordingly. This could either be favorable or unfavorable both to you personally and your business. Know that perception in business is everything!

You are (or supposed to be) an authority in your business and hopefully your family, so model the right behavior of civility to help your family as well as your business associates and show respect when you have any form of communication with them online.

Make sure you maintain courtesy even among members of the family online so that you can maintain some level of civil communication that will not turn off current and future business associates.

Although it may not be a pleasant topic to discuss, it is still important to talk about it because you must always show maturity, self control and professionalism in all that you do as a serious professional. When it comes to past relationships like the former spouse or intimate partner, maintain civility and politeness at all times as in any other situation. You have the right to turn down the invitation if you do not feel comfortable being friends on the social networking sites with a former spouse or intimate partner. Simply send a concise note telling him or her why you believe it is in the interest of both sides to avoid any contact on the social networking sites. Each must respect the other's privacy and accept the outcome.

However, if you do decide to accept the "friendship", try to make it as normal and civil as possible. Don't be tempted to search for information on the new "lucky" partner and what activities your former spouse or intimate partner is now into.

Existing Friends: The temptation to invite all your friends whose email addresses are in your address book should also be avoided. Whereas that can be very convenient, as a professional, you should desist from taking that step and rather seek persons—including your existing friends—or organizations that support your business venture. What is more, it is more polite to send individual messages to your existing friends rather than sending a mass invitation to all.

Knowing the etiquette for making friends, especially online or social networking sites, will help you to nurture your friendships and make them rewarding in the long term.

Making new friends: The opportunity for making new friends has never been easier than it is in social networking today. All it takes is a little effort to create rewarding and satisfying relationships. As a professional, you want to make sure that in any friendship you engage in on any of the social networking sites, you make it a point—as part of your goal in joining the site—to genuinely connect with people, care about serving others, always thinking about ways you can add value to your friends' lives and thereby build true friendships.

Meeting new people on social networking sites means going a step further than just clicking on the friend-request button. It means seeking out the people you believe can benefit from you and you from them. In other words, in connecting with others to create friendships, be real and authentic at all times. You must have at least one thing in common that can gradually help you both build a mutually beneficial relationship.

In proper etiquette, it is good to have something of reference to talk about with somebody you meet for the first time, and this is even more critical in social networking where the person does not see you face-to-face. The best way to start a meaningful conversation is with people whose blogs you read from time to time, those you meet at seminars, people you generally respect for one reason or the other, old classmates and co-workers, authors of books you have read and like and of course any other live networking events you may have attended. This might sound very obvious and yet is often overlooked, especially when professionals begin to engage in social networking. Most of the time, it is the result of not knowing how to start the conversation.

However, that should not be the case if you know the right etiquette to start those conversations to win these people as friends on social networking sites.

In the "Business Etiquette for Dummies", a book by my mentor and friend Sue Fox, good conversationalists all share the following abilities:

- They know how to give and accept compliments gracefully.
- They can talk about many different subjects and are able to maneuver without difficulty through conversations pertaining to things they know little about.
- They can quickly discern potential topics of interest to any given group and steer the conversation in that direction.
- They don't repeat gossip.
- They never correct another person's vocabulary or grammar.
- They know when to discuss business and when not to.

- They involve everyone in the group in conversation, not just one person.
- They know how to step in to fill in an embarrassing void in conversation.
- They have a good sense of humor and are able to relate stories well.
- They can sense when they are boring people.

The point here is to avoid sending a blank friend-request to these people, but to do it in a way that makes you stand out in order to catch their attention. Nothing will do it better than knowing how to start a meaningful conversation in the first place.

Generally, there isn't a single way to start a conversation with anybody in real life situations, let alone when it comes to social networking. It always depends on the person you are dealing with and so it is advisable to be very careful how you start any conversation. It does not however mean that you must avoid starting one all together.

Say for example you want to initiate a conversation and make friends with someone you may have met at a seminar or a networking event. Taking the attributes of proper etiquette and a good conversationalist into consideration, you can confidently and gracefully start to talk about the event you both attended—about the food, drinks, host and how the whole event was run with compliments. Make sure to avoid talking about all the embarrassing incidents that may have happened there or gossiping that may have circulated. For an author you intend making friends with, you can initiate the conversation with a compliment on the quality and value of the book to you personally.

Such tactics make you even more irresistible and encourage the person to accept your friend-request because he or she wants to hear more of what you have to say about their blog posts, their book, or whatever topic you have initiated.

Nonetheless, it is worth pointing out that the way you initiate any conversation will determine which direction that friendship will go.

So reading someone's profile and determining that he or she is someone you would like to make friends with does not only mean clicking the friend-request button.

When making friends, it is advisable to give the potential friend a little background of yourself and to say why you became interested in them in the first place. Such little notes attached to your invitation make you stand out from the rest, already engage the potential friend's attention and break the ice for both of you to start a conversation even before he or she accepts your invitation.

Let's face it, no seasoned professional will attend any live event and immediately insist on being friends with a stranger. Most probably, this other person will call the security right away!

What is more, by adding an extra note to introduce yourself at this early stage does not only show proper social etiquette, but also paves the way for starting genuine conversations that show your honest interest in knowing the other person better and gradually building a relationship that results in a win-win situation.

This emphasizes the above point that, as a professional person engaging in social networking, there is no need to rush in confirming any friend-requests.

Imagine being at a real life networking event and you are approached by a stranger who simply tells you, "be my friend!" I am sure you would wonder if all is well with this person. If you are kind and patient enough, you may ask the person why you should be his or her friend. Yet in the online world, this happens very often. So it really is up to you to decide whether you want to find out more about this person requesting your friendship and to know if it is worth it for you to accept the friendship at all.

You might receive a request from someone you do not know at all. This happens a lot in the online world. For example, from those who do not add any introductory message (and there are a whole lot of them) to those who mistakenly click the send button before having the chance to add the message. Keep in mind, there may be people among them you feel attracted to by just seeing their photograph, for instance, and would want to accept the friend-request.

In such cases, it is very advisable to find out something about them to make sure they are the kind of people in whose company you will like to be seen. It is important that they will have a positive impact or influence on you personally and professionally just like you would have on them. Dennis and Wendy Mannering posed an important question: "Attitudes are contagious. Are yours worth catching?"

Remember, birds of the same feather flock together and the more appropriate people you make friends with, the better your chances are in appropriately branding yourself and reaching your goal of being a successful professional. Fortunately, the internet has made it very easy to find out more information about people we are interested in. Simply by entering the name of the prospective friend into Google Search can elicit enough information to help you make a decision about accepting their friendship or not. It also helps you to know on which note to start a conversation with them.

Of course, there is more to friendship than just liking a picture. Having an idea about the prospective friend helps you not only to avoid any blunders in your interactions but also means that you gradually get to know the person better as you forge ahead in the friendship.

The more your aims and ambitions are aligned with people you are friends with, the more you are able to help each other and work together or alongside each other to achieve your goals as professionals and consequently for your general well-being.

So if someone sends you an invitation and you are not sure if you should accept the request because there was not enough information provided, it is only good etiquette to send this individual a message asking for a little more information about themselves or to simply 'google' them to find out more about them. There is nothing to be shy about, simply let the person know that you intend to network with like-minded people. Simply put, think quality not quantity. It increases your chances of becoming profitably branded!

The etiquette of invitation is a two-way street. When you receive the response from your new friend indicating that he or she has accepted your friend-request, it doesn't end there. You now want to build on the friendship that has just began. One of the many ways of doing so is sending a thank-you note for the acceptance and a follow-up message as an attempt to get to know him or her better. And please use only open-ended questions in your conversation so that you get a better response and something to build on from the clues of the responses sent to you.

Remember, friendship is not just saying "yes, you are my friend". It means getting together from time to time and getting to know each other better to build a meaningful relationship that allows you to support each other.

It really is bad manners and bad professional etiquette to accept a friendship and not do follow-ups. Of course there are times you make the effort to follow up but the other party does not respond. In that case, you must not really worry too much or send too many messages. Up to three messages will be enough because if the other party is really serious about furthering the relationship, he or she will at least send a letter of acknowledgment to let you know that you are still on their mind.

I have personally had instances like these. What I do is to pause for a couple of months and make contact again. If the person still does not respond, then I know for sure this is not a person who really wants to build a meaningful relationship with me. So I end the friendship or just accept them as one of those "dormant" friends.

Another critical behavior that many take for granted is not addressing their new friends with their full names in the initial stages of the friendship. Of course you want to build a great relationship which is not so rigid and very formal. However, it is better to start slowly and not assume that you have the "right" to call people by their first names. Different cultures have different ways of doing things and it could be that it includes addressing someone with their title no matter how close you are to that person. So when addressing a friend for the first time, use their full name plus a title.

Then ask for their permission to call them by their first name or whichever name you wish to call them. After that, you can go ahead and start calling them by the name agreed on.

However, if you do not receive any response as to how to call the person, see what name the person signs off with in his or her communication with you and use that name to refer to them in case they do not respond to your request to call them by a particular name.

Let's face it, a very savvy professional knows that good etiquette demands you properly address a person you are seeing for the first time and that means with all titles and credentials until you are asked to do otherwise. It is no different with online first-time meetings. Sadly, a majority of social networking members overlook this.

I believe if you want to set yourself apart in this over-crowded medium let alone get noticed by the relevant people, not only is it the proper and strategic way to start a friendship but also a foundation for the know-like-trust factor in all your friendships and that is priceless. It always pays to show respect and consideration to others and get to know them one step at a time. It is only then that you can create quality friendships.

Chapter 9

YOU KNOW ME AND
I KNOW YOU, NOW WHAT?

The ability to keep a relationship going is an attribute that many people do not possess and it is even worse in the case of many professionals especially when it comes to social networking.

Note here that being accepted by enough social networking friends to whom you can sell your products or services is not enough in itself. Rather, that is when the real work of social networking begins—building a mutually beneficial relationship that lasts, as mentioned several times already.

That is why you have to respect yourself and others on the social networking sites. This means that you must try at all times to communicate ONLY in a way that makes your friend feel comfortable. If a friend refuses to continue with a particular topic, respect that and avoid raising that topic in future communications.

Please make an effort to avoid renaming your friends. By no means must you assume that you know the short form of a name, so you would rather use that to write or call your friend. Most people will not appreciate that and it is understandable. If you really want to call someone else with a nickname or in some other way, simply asking permission is a great way of showing care and respect.

I have a friend on *facebook* who complained for some time about his friend deciding to give him another name instead of his real name. He was very angry about it. I therefore asked him to make the person aware of his feelings but he told me he had corrected him twice without any positive feedback. So I asked him to write a message to his friend explaining how he feels about the whole situation and that he doesn't see it helping the relationship to advance. How that ended, I have no idea. What really matters now is that you learn to accept people's opinion and respect your friends. This is one of the basics of proper etiquette.

Likewise, it is not polite for you to stop being friends with the other person if you are renamed. It is possible that your friend just did not mean any harm and wanted to become a little bit closer to you to strengthen your friendship. If it happens to you and you are not comfortable with anyone "re-branding you", then the simplest thing to do is to write to your friend to explain and correct him or her. The number of times you are prepared to correct your friend until he or she gets it is really up to you should it continue for more than three times.

Personally, I have had people give me various versions of what they want to call me. Most of the time, I correct them politely and they understand me. One time I had a new friend who made a similar mistake. When I corrected him, he took it so well we ended up having other things to talk about. The "name" topic in fact took our friendship to a new level and made our relationship even stronger.

Chapter 10

BUILDING MUTUAL RELATIONSHIPS

In order to build and make any relationship mutually beneficial so no party feels dominated or cheated, it is always good to start with the Golden Rule: Treat others as you would want them to treat you and, better still, how they would want to be treated. When you do that, you build the reputation of being a friend worth having and sticking around with and you imprint your brand in hearts.

Building mutually beneficial relationship entails a lot of patience, love, care, understanding and open-mindedness. As they say, you've got to "think outside the box!"

Every individual on any social networking site has his or her own world and would do anything to protect it unless you are convincing enough to win them to your side.

Especially on social networks where most friends do not get the chance to meet physically, it is in your own interest as a professional to know how to deal with people from all walks of life with whom you want to build a meaningful friendship. They already have their way of doing things and are usually not prepared to have anyone invade their freedom. That is why it is very important that you proceed cautiously with the friendships you make online.

Avoid being too dominating and gradually find ways and means of learning more about your friends before posting on their walls or spaces. Much as you may not fully understand your friends, it is all about making a positive friendship. So after being accepted as a friend or accepting a friend-request is the time to start finding out about your friends and what their interests are in order to avoid offending them in any way.

Some of the ways to keep the conversation going is by asking your friends what other interests they have apart from what you see on their profile. Try to construct conversations that get your friends involved while getting to know them better, thus building better friendships. You may use the guidelines for a good conversationalist to avoid any blunders. It is also very important to act as you would in real life situations. In other words, be authentic!

You see, just because you are in the privacy of your home in front of your computer does not mean that people are not going to connect your online communication to your personality. So it is always advisable to be your best self because your actions in any social media setting are—more often than not—the direct and only way people perceive you.

Make your primary aim of being in a networking community, first and foremost, relationship-building. Don't rush into telling your new friends how fantastic your business or product is. The idea behind these social networking sites is to create a networking environment and, honestly, that is what ideally any social networking is all about.

However, it does not mean that you cannot join some sites that are strictly for business. *Ecademy, LinkedIn* and *StartUp* are some of the sites that are strictly business oriented and allow you to start talking business right from the beginning if you deem it that urgent. But again, my advice is to first join, take some time to study how things are done right in that particular setting and—when you are confident that you understand their language—step on stage and start your show.

I recently joined a group of professionals online and right from the time I set up my profile page, I got members posting their business opportunities on my wall.

I was shocked but, as usual, decided to study the group before taking any action. I eventually got to know that it is the group's style—which seemed to be too pushy to me—but I am now using that to my advantage by building meaningful relationships with all the people there at the push of a button without selling anything and it is working so great.

This also means that you should not take the leniency of these sites to be their weakness.

First start slowly and understand the etiquette of the group well before making any moves.

Remember to present yourself in any situation first as someone who wants to build a friendly and cordial relationship and then, when the time is right, present all that you have to show. That is exactly what you must consider as well in the virtual world. Let things flow naturally.

Make sure you mean what you say to your friend. Being honest is a virtue that always wins. With so many small businesses springing up every day and engaging in fraudulent acts, you want to set yourself apart as a person worth knowing and doing business with. The level of trust in other people these days is very minimal, so build trust in your online and offline friends.

Most people I have been interacting with just tell me plainly that they do not consider their online "friends" to be real friends when they accept them. It is only when they see their online activities over a period of time and interact more that they develop a true friendship with them.

Honestly, most online professionals build a following of people to leverage their businesses. For that matter, the word SPAM has taken on a new meaning for internet users.

What is more, people really do not care about you until they read and see interesting things about you. They then slowly start getting attracted to you and that is when you gradually win their trust as long as you strike a cord in them. In that sense, it is only good etiquette to mean what you say and say what you mean and also maintain consistency in all you do on the online social networking sites.

Be fair in your actions. Do not treat your friends in any way you would not like them to treat you, or have requested them not to. This does not create a stable relationship and puts your friends in an uncomfortable situation because they never know what to expect from you. In fact when bad comes to worse, some friends may simply stop the friendship altogether.

Don't be egotistical and too proud. Yes, you have to make your friends know what your beliefs and values are but that does not make it right to step on people's toes and believe you can get away with it. Hence, learn to apologize when you go wrong! You possibly think you did not do anything wrong, but if you realize that people read different meanings into things you say and do, then comfortably "wear their shoes" and try to understand why they react.

As humans, we sometimes get angry with and wonder at the behaviour of some people. However, if we will take the time to find out why they behave in such ways, we tend to understand them better and consequently know how to react towards them in a way that does not hurt the relationship or the impression you may have of them.

This also means that should you step on somebody's toes and you are made aware of it, do not take it to heart but be quick to put your pride aside and genuinely apologize in order not to hurt the relationship. After all to err is human and it is only when you have an open mind and are ready to accept other people's opinion that you are able to deal with the various types of people you encounter, especially as a professional on the social networks.

Always realize and keep in mind that doing business with people from other countries also means learning to adjust to their way of doing things. In other words, be tolerant to people of other cultures regardless of whether you are interacting with them online or offline. The fact that you might all be online does not mean that your way must be the highway. Different cultures do things, especially business, in different ways. That is what you must also have in mind when transacting business with them on the social networks.

Another way of cultivating a better friendship on the social networks is by posting meaningful and useful updates on your profile status. The fact that you are allowed to type in anything you want on your status does not mean anything that comes to mind.

Being too opinionated is one way people can irritate their friends, especially when it comes to politics and religion. It is better to be more constructive and look at all angles of the issue you want to talk about than to point fingers at the others. You might not know which of your friends is a republican or a pagan and you sometimes don't need the name "Al Qaida" to eventually form an opinion about a particular friend.

One attribute of proper etiquette is the ability to listen. This does not mean just sitting quietly and reading what other people say to you but also what valuable contributions you bring to the conversation. That is exactly what many professionals and entrepreneurs fail to do with their social networking connections. Do you listen well to your friends?

If you understand your friends' needs, you are able to grow a mutually beneficial relationship that makes everyone a winner.

In today's multicultural world with advanced technology, it is only savvy as a professional or entrepreneur to leverage all possibilities to reach a larger audience in your target market—and you can do that with any social networking platform.

However, it is not necessarily having a large number of friends that matters. Being able to stand out and get an edge over the competition with exceptional performances means you must go a step further to understand the behaviors of your social networking friends as individuals and why they will react to certain issues in a particular way.

Clearly, although we now operate in a global village, individuals still guard and cherish their beliefs and values and will do anything within their power to protect and defend them. And that transcends the way people make their decisions. For this reason it is important to avoid any stereotyping and try to know your friends in order to exhibit professionalism, thoughtfulness, respect and appreciation.

What any serious and focused friend on any social networking platform is looking for is someone they can connect with, who they believe sees them as an individual and understands their needs, is ready and willing to go that extra mile to help them and make the friendship special. Therefore, the preparation of understanding your friends in order to get their clear picture and what makes them choose you over another person is very vital.

If you are able to identify and understand the individuality of your friends, you enhance your experiences and build the necessary trust in them.

When commenting on your friends' photographs, for example, never make remarks or jokes about their gender, body parts or sexual preferences. Show respect and make only constructive comments that strengthen your relationship. If you have nothing to say, don't just type something for the sake of it. This is completely rude.

In the Ghanaian society, there is a saying that—literally translated into English—"The stick used to hit X will also be used to hit Y." It simply means that how a person treats another is how that person will treat you too.

Avoid making negative statements and comments over any medium about the last company you worked with to your friends. You don't have to lie, but avoid slandering your last employer. Even if you hated your job, it is not a good reflection on yourself to spread negative information about your last employer on any social media or elsewhere.

I recently read about a girl who got fired from her job in the United Kingdom because she was telling her friends on a social networking site how much she hated her job. When her former manager was interviewed, he stated it was better for her to look for a more fulfilling job if she was not happy. I certainly agree with him! I nonetheless pity the girl because for a while, she has to be jobless and without any income. Hopefully, she has people to help her out. On the other hand, she has created a stigma for herself and many employers will think twice before employing her because they are not sure what impact she will have on the company if they do employ her.

What some people do not seem to realize is that your personal attitude and brand DOES affect your overall business or the company you work for. It is simply bad etiquette to speak negatively about your partner, company or anything especially in a public setting.

If you do not like your job, keep it to yourself and avoid damaging your reputation with negative utterances. Nobody wants to do business with or employ a person who is always complaining or sending negative information. It simply is not good for business.

On the flip side, should you find yourself in a situation where someone wants to hear such negative information from you, avoid such discussions at all costs. Say, for example, you are not aware of such situations or that you think talking about something else would be better and divert the topic to something more general and positive. Some people are just incurable gossips or test your manners. Therefore, always beware and show maturity and proper manners and etiquette to build the right reputation you need to advance in your business or career.

Another way you can build mutually beneficial relationships with your friends on the social networks is by being discreet and decent in posting comments and messages on your network. Consider what the feeling and reaction of your friends will be before taking that action. Your first question to yourself must be "would this be entertaining, beneficial, relevant and educational to my friends?"

As far as I know, almost all the social networking sites prohibit obscenity or any offensive content on their sites yet some people still take the plunge. Possibly because they do not read the sites' rules and regulations when they join. Whatever the case may be, unless you are in a group that allows such content, always think about the recipient.

My principle is—put out what you believe would positively benefit and/ or entertain your friends.

In my time on any social networking site, I try as much as possible not to send any message, be it text, links, applications, pictures or videos without first considering what my reaction would be if I were the recipient and what the repercussions will be for me as well.

Sometimes, just to be on the safe side and to avoid doing anything adverse, I rather stay away from posting anything at all. Thus, I do not make any contributions to offend anybody. So if you have nothing to say, say nothing!

When you have nothing to tell or anything kind or meaningful to say, do not comment or post on your friends' walls. That is good etiquette because then you neither offend people nor do you make them feel uncomfortable. All you do in this instance of being silent is (again) silently showing them your respect.

Needless to say that despite all the caution, I have also sometimes offended people. This is normal and can happen because you cannot tell what mood a friend may be in when they receive your message, pictures or videos or what meaning they read into what you send them. At that moment, although to you what you shared was not harmful or promotional, it may come across in that way to your friend because of the meaning he or she reads into it. That is when you have to suppress your ego and pride and apologize to your friend for the assumption you wrongly made. That certainly will not make you a lesser human being. On the contrary, it will show your maturity and professionalism and further strengthen your personal brand.

Make sure you first seek the permission of your friends or family members any time you are about to post their videos and pictures and you are not sure about their reaction to seeing their pictures online. This is to ensure that you have their go-ahead before making their images public.

I have heard friends complain that their old-time pictures, which they would otherwise have not made public, were posted by some people. This mostly results in quarrels, suspicion of character and a breakup of the friendship.

Sometimes it feels great to want to tease a friend or a colleague a little on his or her "old look" or to show them that you still have copies of that wild-party picture you took of the two of you both smoking the "thing" and drinking that bottle of Jack Daniels. After all, how many people can afford a Jack Daniels, right? Wrong?!

What you might not know is, after all these years that you have not been in contact with this friend, he or she might have had a change of mind and would rather not have anything to do with those past behaviors anymore. So please contact that old friend before you start making that public album to "share" those pictures or videos.

All social networking platforms are very public places and in no matter how well you know somebody and want to share a picture or a video of you together, it is only proper etiquette that you seek first and foremost, the person or persons' consent before doing that. Simply put, please act more mature and understanding before taking those actions to save the friendship that is being built or that has been rekindled after long years of silence.

With their consent, you are showing them that you respect their privacy and would not do anything against their will. And that's what good friends are for—protecting each other's interests and showing respect for one another.

When it comes to minors, please first ask the parents concerned. Even if it is your own child, let your partner be aware of what you intend to do before posting the video or picture in question. This is the least you could do to show your respect to these individuals.

I remember when I first started joining social networking sites and wanted to post picture of my family, my husband's initial reaction was a resounding NO!

I accepted it but gradually made him understand that as a Brand strategist and a Preferred Lifestyle ambassador as well as an etiquette expert teaching people how to profitably get branded and to live quality lives which includes good manners and etiquette, it is my duty to show them that I walk my talk and live it.

After thinking about it for a while, since he is also convinced that I should help people with my expertise, he finally agreed.

So I am now freely allowed to post images of my family although he controls what image of his I put out there.

Another instance concerns when my little sister (who also is the shy type) visited us some time back.

The fact that she is my sister and I honestly knew she would not object to my posting her pictures online, I did my part by being respectful enough to ask for her consent before posting her pictures in my online albums on the social networking sites I belong to since she is not on any social networking platform. She wholeheartedly agreed! By all means post images that you know the parties involved would not mind seeing online.

No matter how well you think you know somebody, people can sometimes be very funny. So it is always good to play it safe.

Some respected online and social media experts even suggest having a documentation of the agreement but in order not to make life complicated more than it already is, simply use your discretion and do things that are safe both for your personal and professional reputation.

Chapter 11

COMMUNICATING PROFESSIONALLY— THE DO'S AND DON'TS

As much as possible, as a professional using social networking platforms for business, keep a positive tone of communication. People are prone to avoid someone who is overly negative and hostile. If you are naturally a well-mannered person, you tend to avoid very negative and hostile people especially in public places. This is no different in the online world.

In my early days in social networking, I had the privilege of making friends with one famous internet marketer who had a reputation for doing exceptional work. Since I needed help in that area in my business, I employed this person's services. Unfortunately, it turned out that this person's exceptional work did not extend to good manners and etiquette let alone business.

Much as I tried to be calm to avoid making this person feel guilty about the sluggishness of getting the job done, I received hostile, negative and confrontational messages as though I was personally responsible the work wasn't being done. The fact is that I even paid in full before the job was even started. I also made sure that I provided any information that would facilitate the work being done punctually and appropriately. In all that, it turned out that this person simply did not seem to care but enjoyed receiving my money.

As an etiquette expert, I made a conscious effort to avoid any communication that could lead to direct confrontation with this person because I was not prepared for an endless exchange of hostile messages of any sort. In the end, the job was well done as I had expected. I have even recommended this person to other friends who saw the results of the work done. After all, this person does good work, so why not. Don't we all deserve a second chance?

As a professional, note that arguments in any form, even on the internet, can sometimes escalate into ugly exchanges. As such, be very careful not to falsely assume anything even in friendly situations where you frequently exchange messages.

Always make sure before you hit the "send" button, you have asked yourself a couple of times if you would honestly say the same words to the person face-to-face. If yes, send the message but if your answer is even a silent "no", delete the message immediately and rethink before retyping.

It doesn't matter if you have to retype it a hundred times before sending. Make sure you type it in such a way that you would feel comfortable saying it to the person face-to-face.

Always remember that as a professional, your personal brand and reputation are always at stake. Since reputation is king these days, you don't want to compromise it at all.

Always write plainly and clearly in order for your friend(s) to understand you well and give you the correct response or answer.

As you may know, there are times when you just happen to take things for granted and assume that what you intend to put across will be understood the way you would like it to be. This happens especially when you get used to doing things in a particular way and believe others must be familiar with that way as well. However, that is not the reality. All of us still want things to be spelled out for us and made as simple as possible. And that is just normal and understandable for social networking because we are all from different backgrounds and cultures and will understand things in different ways. So really, you ought to be as clear as possible in making your communication meaningful in order to get the appropriate response or reaction.

People do not see your body language or the emphasis you make on particular words and even if they do, different cultures have different meanings for different body languages so it is better to be very clear in your typing. In real life for example, shaking the head may mean disapproval in most cultures but to Indians, it is a sign of agreement. For this and other reasons, it is only good etiquette to always recheck your message before you press the "send" button. If you want the other person to know you meant to be lighthearted, you can use a smiley to illustrate your mood. This is only good as long as you are socializing. However, if the conversation gets serious and formal and you find yourself talking business, avoid emoticons all together!

And if you believe what you are about to send will be too long and complicated then politely ask the other person's telephone number and speak personally with him or her. That will even help you to take your friendship to another level.

Another mistake some professionals continually make is the use of all uppercase letters in their messages. It just looks very unprofessional, lazy and IT GIVES THE IMPRESSION THAT YOU ARE SHOUTING at the recipient. A mixture of both upper and lower case letters at the appropriate places show your professionalism and care.

Also very important is using easy-to-understand words, checking your tenses and making sure what you are trying to put across is exactly what you mean. The computer's spelling check is helpful but sometimes you might type a word that is correct for the computer but probably different from the word you intended to use. That can alter the meaning of your message completely. An example could be that you intended to type 'sole' instead of 'soul' or 'you're' (the short form of 'you are') instead of 'your' (a possessive pronoun), a mistake many professionals make.

In your rush to get the message out, you may overlook these faults. Since the editing application doesn't alert you on any word mistakes, you press "send" not knowing you have distorted your message.

It is therefore very important to know some vocabulary and to double-check if what you intended to state in your messages is what the recipients will read and understand.

Also, long winding messages most often miss the point. That is why it is best to keep your message short and straight to the point while maintaining the meaning.

On the other hand, it is very tempting to be a self-righteous person who corrects all the other people's mistakes. Remember everyone makes mistakes and you can never tell when it will be your turn next time for someone to consistently correct you.

However, should you find it necessary to correct a friend of any consistent mistake, it is advisable to send a separate and private message ONLY to your friend and avoid the temptation of making those corrections publicly.

Being a professional and behaving like one means you must be well informed about your profession and things that will take you to the next level in your career. That is why knowing some internet and chat terms is also very important for your career. A word of caution here: the internet vocabulary might seem to be similar to real-world words, so you must be very careful not to misappropriate them.

On the other hand, in order not to act in ignorance, it is always good to have some internet vocabulary at your finger tips. Not only does it show that you are professional and up-to-date with technology, it also makes communication easier for you and those message recipients who love internet vocabulary.

An example is knowing what *spamming* really means in order not to become a victim of your own ignorance. One site I recommend in case you want to know more about internet vocabulary and terms is *Netlingo*. This site has a dictionary of internet vocabulary.

Also, respect other people's time on the internet. Although the internet is a fast means of communication, people have more important things to do than waiting for your messages.

What is more, they are better off reading meaningful and productive messages than having to waste their valuable time reading messages that are copied (Cc) to all friends in your email list.

Remember that the people on the social networking sites are there to make friends and to network. Much as some will not mind you and ignore the message, others will, out of politeness, open the message only to find it meaningless and a waste of time. Although it might seem very easy and tempting to do, avoid copying all your friends on messages and show them some consideration and respect by sending them individual messages that are personal and meaningful.

Do not expect to receive a response instantly or as soon as you send out a message to a friend. Your friend also has other things to do and will respond in the appropriate time depending on the priority deemed for your message.

Although internet connections have improved dramatically in recent times, there are still slow and unstable connections in some parts of the world. Such circumstances may cause your friends not to respond as fast as you might expect them to.

In order not to waste their time as well, it is worth repeating that your messages should be short and precise as well as clear and understandable. Long messages can get boring and all your friend probably wants to know is what precisely you want to say. Therefore avoid long winding messages—something that I sometimes am guilty of in my excitement to give out information. What this means to you as a professional is to "get straight to the point"!

Should you receive a message that is not clear to you, reply and politely ask for clarification.

Do not assume the meaning of the message and reply in a way that could unintentionally hurt your relationship or send the wrong message. You need to be very descriptive in your writing in order to make your friend understand the emotions and the true meaning of your messages. Remember, they cannot see you.

I once wrote and shared a note with some friends on a social networking site I belong to. After reading the note, a friend commented that I made him feel like he was in the particular situation I described in the note. That is how well you want to make your friends understand your messages.

Communication is not all about formulating words to form a sentence. It is about making those words understood exactly the way you intended them to be and, most importantly, triggering the right emotions in them. This explains why gestures and body language help so well in face-to-face communication.

Online communication on the other hand has its downside because the person you send the message to cannot tell the mood you were in when you typed the message. Likewise, you also cannot predict in what condition your message finds the recipient, thus the need for you to be very descriptive when sending messages via the internet. You might underestimate it, but you cannot imagine how a single word can mean different things to different people.

Respond as promptly as possible to your messages when your friends send you messages or you receive invitations. This shows you are committed to your friendship and are up-to-date with your account and what is happening around you. Certainly if you are unable to respond earlier, it is always good to give a little explanation as to why you could not respond at the time. It is just good etiquette and makes your friends know you did not ignore them but that something did not allow you to respond promptly. Of course with so many friends, it is likely you might overlook some of the messages. Do your best to respond to your messages and—should you miss any—apologize to the friends and give them the necessary response to their message.

When you give a time-frame as to when you will reply fully to a message, make sure to honor it. In this way, you gain even more of your friends' respect and continue to maintain a good reputation. There is nothing as unprofessional as saying you will respond at a certain time and you don't. If you are still unable to keep the agreed time, send a short message to postpone the reply and give a little explanation.

Of course you have to consider the implications of using abbreviations, slang and jargons. If you are on a platform to nurture relationships that could lead to business, it is very important to think about the implications and how this can affect your business and your professional appearance when doing business.

Imagine being in the midst of people with a totally different culture altogether for the first time and they are saying things that you totally have no idea about. You may feel hurt if some of the words sound like insults or attacks. And that is what others feel like when they have no idea about the slang and jargons you use when networking with them, especially when you are doing business. However, the internet and online social networks have their own language. It is wise to be familiar with it in order not to feel like a stranger.

It is only good etiquette that before you visit a new country of interest, you read or do some form of research about that country in order not to feel too out of place when you get there and that includes learning a few words of the local language. And so is it with social networking. It has its own language that you need to have some idea about if you want to feel at home on any of the platforms.

It is important to note at this point that although it is completely bad etiquette to use jargons, slang, acronyms and abbreviations in any form of offline business communication, they give you an edge in social networking, make you look internet-savvy and help you to put across a lot in few words as long as you know your friend understands some internet language. The important thing is to avoid over-using them in your communication.

It is therefore good for a business owner or professional engaging in social networking to have an idea of some of the internet acronyms used these days, especially in business forums.

Certainly, as you nurture your social networking relationships, you can use some of these internet acronyms on the social level. Until recently when much longer messages were allowed, on twitter, all it took was 140 characters to say what you have to say.

Just to give you a crash course on internet business language, I have listed acronyms that you might be familiar with or can take note of. They are used very often in social networking as well as business chat rooms, text messaging, newsgroups and even emails and I hope these will get you well started:

- AFAIC: As far as I'm concerned
- AFK: Away from keyboard
- ASAP: As soon as possible
- BAK: Back to keyboard
- BBL: Be back later
- BD: Big deal
- BFN: Bye for now
- BHAG: Big hairy audacious goal
- BOHICA: Bend over here it comes again
- BRB: By the way
- CLM: Career limiting move
- CUL8R or L8R: See you later
- CYA: See ya
- DD: Due Diligence
- DQYDJ: Don't quit your day job
- DRIB: Don't read if busy
- EOD: End of day or End of discussion
- EOM: End of message
- EOT: End of thread (meaning: end of discussion)
- ESO: Equipment smarter than Operator
- FAQ: Frequently asked questions
- FWIW: For what it's worth
- FYI: For your information

- GAL: Get a life
- GDM8: Good day mate
- GMTA: Great minds think alike
- GRD or GR&D: Grinning, running and ducking
- GR8: Great
- GTRM: Going to read mail
- HIOOC: Help, I'm out of coffee
- HTH: Hope this helps
- IAE: In any event
- IAITS: It's all in the subject
- IANAL: I am not a lawyer
- IMNSHO: In my NOT so humble opinion
- IMHO: In my humble opinion
- IYSWIM: If you see what I mean
- IOW: In other words
- KISS: Keep it simple stupid
- LOL: Lots of luck or laughing out loud
- LOPSOD: Long on promises, short on delivery
- MHOTY: My hat's off to you
- MOTD: Message of the day
- MTFBWY: May the force be with you
- MYOB: Mind your own business
- NRN: No reply necessary
- NSFW: Not safe for work
- NW: No way
- NWR: Not work related
- OIC: Oh, I see
- OOTB: Out of the box
- OTOH: On the other hand
- OTP: On the phone
- OTTH: On the third hand
- PBT: Pay back time
- P&C: Private and Confidential
- PMFJI: Pardon me for jumping in
- QQ: Quick question or Cry more
- RFD: Request for discussion
- RFP: Request for proposal
- RSN: Real soon now (which may be a long time coming)

- RTM: Read the manual
- SME: Subject matter expert or social marketing expert
- SITD: Still in the dark
- SOL: Sooner or later
- STD: Seal the deal or Sexually transmitted disease
- TANSTAAFL: There ain't no such thing as a free lunch
- TBA: To be advised
- TBD: To be determined
- TIA: Thanks in advance
- TIC: Tongue in cheek
- TLA: Three-letter acronym
- TTFN: Ta ta for now
- TTYL: Talk to you later
- TWIMC: To whom it may concern
- TYVM: Thank you very much
- WIIFM: What's in it for me
- WOMBAT: Waste of money, brains and time
- WTG: Way to go
- WYSIWYG: What you see is what you get
- YW: You're welcome

If you must send direct personal messages however, it is always good etiquette to avoid all these acronyms, slang and jargons.

It is possible that you might occasionally offend some friends with the use of this internet language, therefore make sure you understand why they are offended. For this reason, it is always good to ask the recipients of your message if they understand all you are putting across. Very, very importantly, it is your duty to make sure that your messages are not misinterpreted.

If you have been using the internet for a while, you may be aware of some of the etiquette rules. Most of them are not different from what you need on the social networking platforms. Simply put, always be considerate to others and see them as the human beings they are and make them feel comfortable in your company by helping them understand you better, no matter what cultural background they have. This does not only help you to build long-lasting relationships but also helps you to strengthen your credibility and to build a powerful brand for yourself and your business or career.

There are certainly situations where etiquette rules may vary from platform to platform but the basic rules still hold for all of them: stay out of conflict, respect yourself and others and try to understand people better because words could have different meanings.

That's why online communication should always be clear. With internet text messages, you unfortunately do not get the opportunity to see the other person's facial expressions, body language or hear their vocal intonations. It is therefore very wise to avoid jokes and any form of communication that you may think is funny because your counterpart might not find it that way at all. If you however know the person very well and are used to such communication, feel free doing so. Still, make sure that the person certainly understands what you mean.

This is what makes a platform like twitter special because you generally only have 140 words to express yourself.

In such cases, you know you must be very brief and that is exactly the same mindset you should have when sending any message on the internet—be concise, straight to the point and stick to the subject of discussion. Also learning how to write on this platform will help you do that without being offensive. So generally, avoid using abbreviations and completely keep slang out of any messages you send out in your professional capacity.

Most social networking platforms are international but it does not mean that as a professional you should be tempted to take things for granted when it comes to communicating with your international friends. So to summarize it, be extraordinarily careful in your communication and dealings if you want to create the right impressions and brand for yourself and your business anywhere you go! However, if all this seems too daunting for you, then stick to the good old-school full sentences but please, don't use phrases like "you must . . ." or "you need to . . ." or any other that sounds controlling. Instead, you might want to try "you can please start by . . ." or "you may want to consider . . ." or "you are welcome to try . . ."

Such phrases put your friends in the decision-making seat instead of making them feel you are trying to be authoritative and dictating to them.

One very important etiquette guide if you are a person who takes alcohol: DON'T drink and type! Sometimes you receive messages from people and wonder if they had a sip of some alcohol before typing the message . . . And that is so true!

I have witnessed friends who I know to be very decent, yet from time to time I read things they post and wonder if they had gulped down some Bacardi!

An example is shamelessly criticizing people who are dear to them and using bad language that under normal circumstances would not come out of their mouths. That is purely bad etiquette and unprofessional. You might never know who will be reading what you post. For all you know, it is your next joint-venture partner or your next well-paying and fulfilling job. What a shame!

On that note, avoid communicating under the influence of alcohol at all times.

Similar to checking your mood, the influence of alcohol could make you send a message that could ruin your personal brand image and reputation.

Always keep in mind that the internet has a very good archive and, therefore, memory.

At the time of typing those messages or posting those pictures and videos, it might be funny but on the flip side, it can be seriously damaging within your professional contacts. So beware!

Also, refrain from flirting with your long-distant social networking friends. It is generally harmless to flirt but you may not know if the person you are trying to flirt with is willing or not. It is better not to begin a professional relationship with a flirt but rather get to know the person. Later when you meet him or her and you still believe you want to be intimate, you may ask for a date and move on from there. Just as in physical life, if you want to maintain your reputation and remain professional and in control of affairs, it is always good etiquette to avoid such acts because you never know who might make or break your career.

On the other hand, if someone flirts with you and you are not in favor of it, you may simply ignore the message or application to flirt back. Yes, interestingly enough, there are applications for flirting! However, if it does go on for a number of times, send a message to let the person know that you would rather prefer to maintain a professional relationship or a normal friendship.

I remember I used to receive massages and "flirting applications" from some guys at the beginning of my social networking. Yes, I have clearly stated on my profile that I am married but that does not seem to tell them anything. I therefore decided to do what is right and sent them, one by one, messages that clearly stated I was happy with my marriage and would not want to start such a relationship anywhere else. One guy actually wrote back and said, it doesn't matter that I am married and that we could do things on the side without my husband knowing. Well, in such an instance, just end the friendship with such a person so you can have your peace of mind and enjoy your sanity.

On the other hand, although I am not encouraging it, if it's your style of having multiple intimate relationships then have your fun.

Chapter 12

MIND YOUR NETIQUETTE
WHEN SOCIAL NETWORKING

Throughout this book, I believe I have adequately emphasized how important your etiquette is when it comes to social networking. I will at this point add that it is equally important to pay attention to your netiquette when you are on any social networking platform or generally as a member of any social networking site. If you are like many professionals trying to maximize the leverage of the social networking platforms, then you might have experienced those moments when you just had to "tweet this news" or "take these pictures and post them as soon as possible" or even "film this scene" to show your "friends."

Well, before you start taking those actions, please check your netiquette first. Simply put, netiquette are the rules of etiquette that govern the internet and the use of new technology.

As a professional or business owner, these include your use of cell phones, pagers, email, iPods, iPads, Flip cameras and so many other electronic devices. Being a business owner or an independent professional aiming to succeed in your business, I am sure—like in all activities you undertake for your business—you try as much as possible to fit many activities into your social networking ventures in order to become more visible to your friends and target market.

In as much as you need to keep maximizing your time, I also hope that you are giving consideration to other equally important issues like the "keep your cell phone off during a meeting!" I expect this statement to generate a lot of divergent opinions. However, that is where the misunderstanding of etiquette starts most of the time.

Although Emily Post may not have had the slightest idea about the possibilities of new technology today, there is one thing she did know for sure that fuels building mutually beneficial relationships: the importance of etiquette in making people feel comfortable in your company or putting them at ease.

"Manners are a sensitive awareness of the feelings of others. If you have that awareness, you have good manners, no matter what fork you use."—Emily Post

There is one very big piece in your business puzzle that you MUST NEVER FORGET in anything you do. It is people who make your business successful and therefore they deserve your attention, recognition and respect.

What I am trying to make you aware of is the fact that just as in any situation in life, the foundation of any success is all about contribution and service to others. Like many professionals, you might have a gadget or two to keep you connected to your work and all the information you need including those from and to your social networking platforms.

Building a business entails several one-on-one meetings with prospective clients or partners.

In such cases, it is always advisable to have all gadgets switched off. It is only good etiquette to give the potential client your full attention rather than constantly excuse yourself for reading your tweets and sending new ones, photographing or making snippets of videos to show your followers and friends. Keep in mind that the golden rule works for everybody. If you would not be happy dealing with a partner who is not concentrated, then don't do it to others.

Honestly, you should never be virtually social networking during a meeting just as you should not be making phone calls—a mistake some so-called professionals still make. Ask yourself why you are about to have that meeting in the first place. If it is to engage in a (business) conversation to share productive ideas, then give your full attention in order to be serious, professional and focused in the discussion at hand. If you have a meeting and tweet or do other social networking activities at the same time, don't be surprised when you don't hear from the person again.

If you MUST do some kind of social networking activities about the meeting, it is only proper etiquette to seek the consent of the other party and better do it after the real meeting is over.

If you really have to carry all those gadgets around, avoid giving the impression of a messy, disorganized person. That means you must be honest and ask yourself if you really need all those gadgets. Your laptop and your cell phone, iPod or iPad may probably not necessarily be worth taking with you to that particular meeting anyway.

If you however "find" enough reasons as to why you need them all—including your video camera—, then try to store them all nicely in one place so that you do not appear to your partner or colleagues as clumsy but rather very much polished, organized and professional. You will also not have to worry about leaving them in a taxi or at the restaurant. That is just the physical part of social networking!

Another social netiquette is being very polite to your net friends in your communication. Anytime I make friends, I try to find out how they got to my profile. It is my way of starting a conversation and fulfilling my curiosity as to why they are choosing me as a friend.

On such two occasions, I had two unpleasant responses from a man and a woman who did not understand why I should ask them such a question. Trying to be my polite self, I explained to them why. The woman is now a good friend. Imagine if I also had been unfriendly to her!

The advice here is to stay level-headed and always be polite.

The world is now a much smaller place than it was years ago, so never answer an insult with another insult. It is great how technology has made communication very easy, yet people don't always understand the right way to utilize it.

It is amazing how some professionals feel so confident in front of their home cameras and return insults to other people who have said something incorrect or bad about their industry, profession or opinion. They even use their Blogs—their proud virtual real estate and 'brand vehicle'—to lash others openly.

As an industry expert, professional or guru, the best way to tackle cases that seem not to conform to your beliefs and opinions is to only provide facts and figures and evidence to prove that what the other person reported is inaccurate. Judgment should be left to the readers, listeners or viewers to make. Avoid being a quarrelsome professional who tries to portray high esteem and confidence at one point and no control at all at another.

Check your mood any time you are sending messages because it affects the tone of your writing.

There are two schools of thought on this. One school believes you cannot be emotional when writing while the other believes you can.

Regardless of whichever side you may be on, my advice is to avoid responding to messages if you feel the response is not flowing as you would like it to or you are not happy or unsure of what signals it will send across. Do so—even if it means postponing the response to a question or message—because it could save your reputation.

What you could do at that very moment is to acknowledge the letter and send the appropriate response on a later date. It is safer to do so than to rush into answering or responding to a message that you will later regret you sent.

You see, human beings experience various emotions at various times and that, to an extent, affects the way you react to others in particular situations when you really do not have self control. Your anger could therefore cause you to negatively react in a message, or over excitement could cause you to say whatever you feel may be fun and great to talk about. The fact that it is an internet message does not mean you must be too relaxed and put your professionalism aside nor does it give you the license to be rude and disrespectful to others when making yourself clear.

It is important to state here that you must stick to the subject and only state your facts in an argument and avoid being too relaxed or self-righteous and a know-it-all.

Many people do not realize it but your mood shows most of the time in your writing as it shows in your body expressions in physical life.

So whether you can show emotions in writing or not is really not what is important. What matters is how you show self-control and respect and consideration for the other person, supposedly your friend. You can never hide who you are!

Also, avoid being political or using strong political stand-points in your social networking communications unless it is in line with your goal. Focus on the business at hand.

Unless you know your friend well and know that he or she will not be offended, never ask questions or make jokes about religion or politics.

Religion is probably the most sensitive of all topics, so keep your focus on why you joined the network and avoid making your friends see you as a critic or rude individual.

Know how to say thank you when someone does you a favor or helps you in anything and never miss the chance to show appreciation to helpful people in any way possible. Remember they are not obliged to give any helping hand and even if they are, it is only good courtesy to show genuine appreciation. It is very interesting how people take this for granted and wonder why they do not make any significant advancement in their careers or businesses.

Human beings by nature like to be acknowledged and appreciated. It is only nice of you to reciprocate at least with a "thank you" when someone does you a favor.

I always keep saying that I have enjoyed many favors in life simply by leveraging simple courtesy. People like it, so use it to your advantage. It works and I can prove it!

The beauty of it all is that the more you appreciate people, the more they tend to help you in whatever capacity they can.

If you discover that a friend has a disability, avoid using words such as "not normal," "disabled," "handicapped," "crippled," or "invalid" to describe him or her when referring to them to other friends or to them personally. Use their correct names. They also need to feel respected and valued as individuals.

Following on the above point, it is also very important to note that for proper etiquette's sake, avoid being so self-righteous! Everyone makes mistakes including you and me. You never know when you will make a mistake. Be very aware that once you criticize someone and try to correct their mistakes, your time will come when you will be put on the radar to be corrected too. Knowing something more than others does not mean you should get personal and lord it over them. When someone makes a mistake,—be it a silly question or an unwanted comment—be kind about it and let it go. It always pays to think twice about correcting someone. It is just not necessary but rather plain rudeness and annoying.

I told you about the internet marketer earlier on whose services I used. I could have sent a direct message correcting all the mistakes with regard to good manners in my capacity as a brand strategist and an etiquette expert, or I could have been kind enough to send a copy of "Etiquette for Dummies" for this person to learn more about proper etiquette but it may have been taken negatively. To avoid all this, I did none of the above.

This did not make me a weakling, rather it reinforced the fact that people are different and that we must respect each other's opinion. So in the process, I learned to respect this person's way of thinking and opinions and how to go about things if I wanted to maintain a mutually beneficial relationship. I therefore made a conscious effort to avoid reacting to all negativity from this person and did what was expected of me in the course of the work being done until eventually, I ended the communication and the topic altogether to maintain peace and my sanity.

After all, it is better to lose money than integrity—something money cannot buy!

Chapter 13

THE ATTITUDE OF GRATITUDE!

According to Lionel Hampton, "Gratitude is when memory is stored in the heart and not in the mind." That is exactly what you want your friends in the social networks to do especially when you want to get profitably branded online. It is very true in our physical world too. Thus, it is kind to thank people the very moment you notice their kindness.

As a professional, a simple message sent to your friend's inbox—or a call if you are well connected—is always welcome when you just want to say how much you have appreciated the kind gesture or words.

Therefore, as Brian Tracy rightly stated, "Develop an attitude of gratitude and give thanks for everything that happens to you, knowing that every step forward is a step toward achieving something bigger and better than your current situation."

Social networks these days even make it easier to show gratitude by using application functions such as the 'like' and 'share' buttons on facebook and the 'retweet' button on twitter. There are other sites where you can even cast a vote and recommend a person or a product to others. All these are ways you can show gratitude to your friends. Nevertheless, this does not mean you must just rely on these buttons because nothing surpasses the good old self-constructed note or message to friends to honestly tell them how grateful you are for their contributions to your activities.

As your friends share your information with their friends, it is good etiquette to thank them personally for their kind gesture if you get wind of it.

Similar to what my friend Herbert Mensah wrote sometime ago on facebook, ". . . just because we don't believe in the laws of gravity doesn't mean we are exempt from them. Similarly, just because you don't know the laws of the universe doesn't mean you aren't subject to their consequences . . ." In reference to Herbert's note, a law that very well applies here is the law of reciprocity!

Simply put, as long as you do good things to your friends, you will surely have your fair share of good karma. Whether you believe it or not, nothing goes unrewarded in this universe!

Therefore, although it might just have been a "retweet", a "like", or a "share" button that your friends clicked, it is always good to comment to acknowledge those actions. If possible, return the favor by doing something similar for them too. That makes your friends appreciate you more and know that you are attentive and kind enough to even thank and acknowledge their deeds. With that, you can only build a stronger relationship and to strengthen the "know, like and trust" factor. As a result, your friendship can only get better and mutually beneficial.

Cultivating the attitude of gratitude is one sure way of gaining a competitive edge over your competition because many people overlook the power of these gestures and just do not pay particular attention to them. Going the extra mile is what will always make you stand out, step up and glow in any situation and make you create that difference between the ordinary and your exceptional self!

"Silent gratitude isn't much use to anyone," says Gladys Brown Stern. William Arthur Ward puts it even better: "feeling gratitude and not expressing it is like wrapping a present and not giving it."

No matter how genuinely grateful you may feel in your heart about your friends' contributions, kindness and help, it means nothing if you do not express it to them!

Therefore, although it is more appropriate to send a well thought out thank-you note, you can for example also reciprocate by clicking the 'like' button on facebook to express your admiration for the kindness accorded to you if you are short of time and words or simply lazy. Practice makes perfect, so let the attitude of gratitude become a part of your everyday actions. Share your gratitude with other friends to let them know how kind other people have been to you on the social network platforms you belong to. It will certainly strengthen and support your friendships.

You see, gratitude is a way of expressing yourself in a positive manner. The more you are consciously thankful, the more you will become happier and fulfilled by attracting positive opportunities into your personal and business life. It really pays off in a big way!

This brings us to our next point—Be generous! This cannot be stressed enough anywhere.

As a business person, you always have to think of how socially responsible you can be at any time. You need not build a community center or provide food for the hungry before you are recognized as being socially responsible. Any social network community is just a place good enough to start being socially responsible by helping those who need your help or providing relevant information which you know would benefit your community. It is also sometimes good for you to research and find out how you can creatively use your knowledge to help people in your networks in a way that is collectively beneficial to all.

Many people are suffering in the world we live in today. There must be a reason why you are gifted with your business idea or profession to be of service to those who badly need it. It is therefore your duty to help those who you are capable of helping.

For sure, you are a professional in business for profits but know that if you refuse to be generous, you will not even have the chance to know how valuable your gift is.

It is only when you are generous by providing free advice, information and gifts that you will know whether what you offer the masses is worth your effort and value in the first place.

In case you haven't thought about it, by being selfless to those who need your help, you are also indirectly conducting an invaluable survey that can greatly have a positive impact on your career or market and set you up for the next level of success.

In the context of business-building mechanics, it is always prudent to survey the target audience to find out what it needs before putting any product or service on the market. Although this is an essential step, we sometimes do not get the people to respond in the numbers that we want.

So why not use "winning through legal bribery" as my very good friend and mentor Joseph Sugarman puts it in his great book "Triggers"?

This subtle method will not only get people to provide you with the answers you want to take your business to the next level but also provide you with qualified ready-to-buy customers who have already made up their minds to purchase your product and do not need any more persuasion.

While you fully concentrate on your professional and business promotion, don't forget to be quick to acknowledge and congratulate your friends when they make any achievements!

There is the tendency to dismiss it as "none of your business," trivial, off-topic or even contrived sometimes. However, these are the little acknowledgments that help to strengthen the relationships you have with the friends in question. This shows admiration of your friends' progress in life and the fact that you recognize them as individual human beings.

So make it a point now to acknowledge your friends' birthdays, weddings, parenthood, retirements, funerals and any events that they share with you on the social networks you belong to.

It is very important to note that much as it might be tempting, refrain from recounting a similar situation you have also been through when sympathizing with or congratulating your friend and let the focus mainly be on the friend alone. It is bad etiquette to talk about your past situation while acknowledging that of a friend.

If you have so much gratitude and want to thank your friends for their concern in case you are the one marking any of these life events, send your friends physical thank-you cards if you feel that is more appropriate considering the level and strength of the friendship you have developed so far.

Making recommendations is another way you can show gratitude to your friends as long as you are confident and sure about their capabilities and know exactly how to formulate the recommendation for people to understand how resourceful the person in question is.

Sometimes you know their capabilities but do not know how well to formulate them to make others understand exactly what and how resourceful that person may be. In this case, it is better not to make the recommendation at all since you might rather be doing more harm than good to your friend. The formulation might sound too good to be true or simply not good enough.

Therefore, in order not to create any blunders, stick to the facts and make it short to the point while taking into consideration the person you are making the recommendation to as well.

Making recommendations is a way to show your friends that you trust them and their capabilities and that you are ready to tell others about their good work and services. How about that for building a mutually beneficial relationship?!

Chapter 14

MY GLOBAL VILLAGE

"Human beings are parts of a body, created from the same essence. When one part is hurt and in pain, the other parts remain restless. If the misery of others leaves you indifferent, you cannot be called a human being . . ."—Sa'adi Shirazi, Persian Poet-Philosopher and Author (1204-1292)

It is for this reason that as a professional engaging in social networking, you in particular must pay attention to two very crucial issues that cut across every nation—religious freedom and geopolitics!

As I stated earlier in this book, being open-minded and showing consideration and respect to other people's beliefs and values is a sure fire to win good friends. This can not be stressed enough in our global village where you might meet people who have strong political or religious points of view. You must try to avoid any instances of being too political or religious on any social networking platform. However, that does not mean that you must suppress your freedom of speech if what you have to say is constructive and void of criticism and assaults that could hurt others. After all, we are obliged by good etiquette to make our friends feel comfortable in our company and that is what you need to aim for as a savvy professional.

Various organizations have been formed to address such issues. With respect to politics, the International Center for Geopolitics Studies (I.C.G.S.) was formed in 2001 to study and analyze the geopolitical problems of the world system in order to better understand the evolution of contemporary international relations. Their activities to-date include addressing general issues on disinformation, economic warfare and religious conflicts.

In regard to religious freedom, the third President of the United States, Thomas Jefferson, and America's founders called it the "first freedom." It is enshrined in the first clause of the first amendment of the United States constitution.

Discussing the reason for religious freedom, The Hudson Institute emphasized how salient religious freedom is today as it was half a century ago and that it allows freedom of thought, conscience, press and association, depending on the prior guarantee of a free conscience. The institute also added that historical reality proves that where religious freedom is denied, so too are other basic human rights.

Much as this is all great information and needed to give us more confidence in our political and religious communication especially on the internet, many are those who have absolutely no idea about their rights and live a life that is truly wanting in order to simply fit into society. His Holiness, Pope Paul VI proclaimed a declaration on religious freedom on December 7, 1965. I selectively quote parts of the declaration http://religiousfreedom. lib.virginia.edu/universal/Dignitat.html:

1. "Many pressures are brought to bear upon the men of our day, to the point where the danger arises lest they lose the possibility of acting on their own judgment . . . Religious freedom therefore ought to have this further purpose and aim, namely, that men may come to act with greater responsibility in fulfilling their duties in community life."

You may agree with me that with the introduction of the internet and especially the influx of social media and social networks, the world has become even smaller than it was a few years ago thus making politics and religion even more sensitive than they were before.

Just as you must know how to behave when you are in the Bronx, you must likewise know how to behave when you are dealing with friends in Bombay, Budaiya or Bukom.

This is even more important when you, as a professional in particular, are dealing with international clients and customers whose only means of contact with you might be the internet. Knowing how to handle yourself on the social networks with dignity and integrity is what will set you apart from your competitors.

Social networking for business on an international level must not be cumbersome. Although some misunderstandings may occur, they must not compromise your integrity.

You just must be prepared for all sorts of characters that you may never understand, considering the fact that many do not take the impact of their actions on others into consideration on social networks in particular and are insensitive to other people's beliefs and values.

It is therefore wise for a professional to take that extra step of reading about your friends' countries of origin in order to understand them better when communicating and to some extent know why they take certain actions differently.

Therefore do not be surprised if some friends contribute less to discussions than others. It could just be a cultural thing whereby they are simply reserved in public settings and would rather avoid being heard too much.

In such a case, if you want more contributions to your input, find out which group of friends feels freer to make comments on your topics and invite them more often to read your inputs. They will love you for being generous and sharing information they like to read.

And don't make the mistake of starting a conversation by asking a French friend personal questions.

Again a word of caution on using jargons: a presentation or action that "bombs" your American friends is something that fails, yet the same "bomb" word used in a similar sentence to your United Kingdom friends will mean a successful venture.

So study what your friends like and what they do not like, what their beliefs and cultural values are. This will help you to start mutually beneficial relationships with your global friends and subsequently get profitably branded for growth and success in your business.

Always realize and keep in mind that doing business with people from other countries means learning to also adjust to their way of doing things. In other words, be tolerant to business people of other cultures regardless of whether you are interacting with them online or offline. The fact that you might all be online does not mean that your way must be the highway. Different cultures do business in different ways and that is what you must also bear in mind when transacting business.

Be sure of showing recognition and respect for your global friends who follow other traditions, religious and political views as well as ways of socializing and doing business.

Also, be very careful of typecasting when communicating with your global friends. Don't assume that all your African-American male friends would like you to refer to them as "Bro" or "Mate" for all your Australian friends and never assume that your Chinese friend can tell you what the year holds for you in the Chinese calendar. Remember, you want to get profitably branded and to leverage the social networking sites to your business advantage.

Chapter 15

SAVVY PROFESSIONALS
TALK ABOUT SOCIAL MEDIA
NETWORKING ETIQUETTE

Murshidah Said

Social media and networking etiquette is indeed important to business people who want to reach out to their target audiences and market. Business people get to brand themselves both online and offline and spread the message that they believe in. In today's business environment, both are interrelated. You cannot do one without the other. However your message, brand and image must be in tandem and congruent with your offline image and etiquette.

Social network can make or break a business deal. In today's wired business and social environment, people are as much online as they are offline. Etiquette online if not done correctly or when you are offensive to your target audience, can cause your image or brand to be affected as a business. Social networking etiquette reflects on how you as a person or a company conduct your business whether it's online or offline and can indeed make or break the deal. I am a big believer of "how you do one thing is how you do verything". Having a good image and etiquette online does affect your bottom line. A good etiquette allows others to know you better and have more trust in you especially when you are open to share with the world about yourself, your beliefs, what you stand for and the products or service that you offer.

Having said that I am a big believer of "HOW YOU DO ONE THING IS HOW YOU DO EVERYTHING", I believe in never ending personal development as the energy in yourself and your thoughts will be released through your choice of words, your comments, your posts and your behaviour online as well.

My personal advice on social networking etiquette: Make sure your business is congruent with the message, posts, comments and beliefs that you carry especially when sharing with your clients, prospects and the world. Always remember how you would react if you were the other person receiving the message that you are giving. Finally, keep improving yourself as the energy in your words and conduct will always be reflected the message that you send out.

Murshidah Said
Director—Training & Events
M & Z Empowerment Center (Co. Reg. 001713640-A)
Suite 33-01, 33rd Floor, Menara Keck Seng,
203 Jalan Bukit Bintang
55100 Kuala Lumpur, Malaysia
http://www.mzempowerment.com/

Becky Cortino

Social networking etiquette is key to establishing meaningful relationships. How it is applied—or not, directly impacts a participant's success.

Etiquette in the realm of social media networking provides a broadly-recognized framework for ethical operating procedures. This code specifies actions and communications that are acceptable within the existing culture.

Observing the conventional standards governing behavior greatly enhances networking efforts. These best practices include requirements for appropriate participation and interaction, to maintain favorable status within the culture, as defined by a specific venue or social media platform.

How a participant relates to others, shares information, and makes connections indicates their willingness to operate ethically and professionally within the scope of a community. While the need to stand out in a sea of others is a well-recognized pillar of personal branding, truly remarkable qualities are clearly communicated when strategic, clever and appropriate actions are thoughtfully taken by a skilled savvy professional.

Becky Cortino,
Marketing-Communications Indie Pro
http://www.ExpressItMediaFusion.com

CONCLUSION

The bottom line is to look at any situation in which you find yourself in the social media. Think of how you would personally react in a similar situation in real life and move on from there with politeness and respect. If you are unsure, let it rest for the time being. Search your heart or find out from a trusted person who you believe can give you a reliable and relevant answer to tackle the challenge and don't forget to find out a lot about various groups of people.

Note that these are not hard and set rules, you are entitled to behave anyhow you want on any social media platform you find yourself and be ready to accept the consequences.

However these are just guidelines to help you present yourself, your brand image, and your professionalism in a more friendly and positive way that will benefit you in the long run—to create a profitably branded business and career on the social media platform in order to attract the right kind of people to you for success in whatever venture you undertake.

After all, the people in these social media are all real people like you and in as much as some of them, well, do not behave right in these media, they still want their fair share of respect and recognition from other people (not fair but true). So since two wrongs don't make a right, and as a professional your aim should be to build a potent brand, it is your duty to maintain your sanity and control and gradually work your way through in a proper manner that will help you reach your aim for joining the club in the first place for becoming profitably branded.

It doesn't mean that you have to be rigid in your actions. Just be yourself but capitalize on the 'good and polite you' to reap better benefits from your social networking efforts. I believe nobody has extra time to waste!

At this point, I would like to introduce two friends who, like good and caring friends do, have agreed to give you their two cents on social media and social networking especially when it comes to the 3 most powerful, must-join, social networking sites on the internet—*facebook*, *LinkedIn* and *twitter*.

So with pride and joy, let me introduce my good friends Terry Brock and Stephanie Ward to you. Please read what they have to tell you with all seriousness and apply them in your business because they simply work!

Social Networking Advice From Two Good Friends

TERRY BROCK:

Social Networking Vs. "Real Life Networking:" Which Is Better?

Business-Building Steps From Terry Brock

I love Social Media and Social Networking! In my audiences where I speak, I see more and more serious business people are devoting time, money and effort to learn how to use these tools. Social Networking tools provide the ability to connect with others in ways that we never would otherwise. By using Twitter, I have connected with people that I would never have met in my normal life. I love Facebook as many "friends of friends" connect where we find common interests. I love YouTube as I've posted over 100 videos about various marketing topics and attract people around the world to see them.

Yet, I hear a conversation that is emerging more and more about the importance of being with real people in real places. Some say that they want a "real" contact. Hey, I understand. When it comes to Relationship Marketing, being available for paying customers and interacting with good people is always important. I personally find that I cherish more and more the quality, non-rushed times when I can be with friends around the world breaking bread, sharing a few drinks or just visiting and catching up with them.

Does this mean that we should throw away our Twitter accounts, "De-Friend" all our Facebook Friends and get rid of YouTube?

Not on your life!

I see it as not "either or, but both and."

When you can connect with new customers at a level of interest and help them, which is great. Each of the social media tools has a unique advantage. I find that focusing on the "Top Four"—Twitter, Facebook, Linkedin and YouTube—help to provide a reasonable connection with others for core business use. Then I use my WordPress Blog to be the focal point to provide value. This strategy is working for many today. It's working for me.

You connect with others in the real world through good old-fashioned meetings (remember those?). Participation in real-world meetings is as essential today as it ever was. We like to meet with people, see them in action, watch their reactions to various events and get to know them. Social Media is never going to replace that and it never tried to. 200 years ago people would get together face-to-face and discuss business and other aspects of life. When the printing press was developed and words could finally be communicated without the use of verbal-only communication, it made human connections better. A few years ago, email was derided as a tool that would diminish human ommunication. It has been used to enhance connections with people but it has to be used properly.

That is the key for marketers today. The tool is not the issue. We often like to make it about the tool. The issue is about your ability to connect with real paying customers in a value-for-value way. As you provide help to them you are able to establish, grow and nurture the relationship.

Whether in person or using the latest, greatest technology tool it is most important to connect with customers. Focus your business efforts on 1) Generating new business and 2) Keeping current customers giddy with glee because they are working with you.

Use current technology to serve customers, but don't ever give up on live, direct connections with others. This happens through phone calls, hand-written letters (yes, they stand out in today's world very well!) and physical face-to-face meetings. As new technologies come and go, it is the people connection that matters more than ever.

Constantly enhance your "people connecting" skills. Go to the networking meetings, seminars, conventions and other gatherings with the mind-set to help others. Contribute value first. After the meeting follow-up using the various tools of communication focusing on the preferred medium of your buyer (phone, email, Twitter, Facebook—whatever!). This combination of the human touch and leveraging technology is a sure-fire winner in any economy!

As a Relationship Marketer, you'll be able to help others—and your own business—the more you focus on being there for other people to meet their needs. Use the tools for what they are meant to be. Focus on people and you will not only do well in business—but also in life.

Copyright © 2009, Terry Brock and Achievement Systems, Inc. *Time Management With Social Media—Don't We Still Have Jobs To Do?*

Business-Building Action From Terry L. Brock

Okay, okay, okay! Enough already! Have you had it with all the "You've got to be on social media" advocates incessantly reminding you that "Twitter is the new E-Mail" or how much you need to be on Facebook, Linkedin, etc. etc.?

But what about the rest of us who have real jobs we need to do? What about those of us who don't want to spend everyday, all day swapping quotes, "retweeting" cute aphorisms, and "linking" with people we don't even know? And hey, Facebook users, I remember a time with being a "friend" meant you actually had MET the person!

Some of us are out there, slaving away in the salt mines, working on such "20th Century" concepts as producing products, meeting with customers and trying to pay the bills. Geez, how did this country ever get started without George Washington, wintering at Valley Forge, letting his soldiers send "tweets" to each other just to pass the time?

Okay, I'm being a little blunt but I think you see my point. What are we to do today with all the deluge of social media "must dos" when we still have work that needs to be done (or at least those who still have a job in this economy!)? What is the proper balance to get the work done, please customers, bring in money—and still be up on the social media explosion that really is changing the way we connect and communicate.

As with so many things in life, there is a balance. And now, the balance is shifting. Here are some suggestions that can help you manage this tidal wave shift in the way we communicate today.

1. **Determine Your Goals.** Have a good heart-to-heart discussion with yourself first, and then with your team around you, what your real goals are in your business. Connecting with people and building strong relationships is undoubtedly a big part of any successful business relationship today. Yes, social media is a vital, critical part of the mix. Just make sure you've got your goals firmly in mind before embracing any new do-dad or gizmo that purportedly "boosts" productivity.

2. **Start With Baby Steps.** Hey, Linkedin wasn't built in a day. Begin with a solid profile for Twitter, Facebook and Linkedin that is other-oriented. Don't talk about yourself as much as the benefits your business provides others. Gradually learn about the protocol of each medium and get to know people. Be a human being first. The sales will follow if you practice Relationship Marketing properly in social media. Always remember that social media and social networking are really about Relationship Marketing.

3. **Get Tools To Facilitate Your Use.** Don't try social media at home—alone. Tools like TweetDeck, HootSuite, Social Oomph and many others really make it easier and much better to use Twitter, Facebook and Linkedin. I'm using these now and they have saved me huge amounts of time. Bonus: Ping.fm and Tubmogul.com can boost your bottom line if you use them properly by sending your best material to lots of places fast.

4.   **Play Well With Others.** The Lone Range was a TV show long ago. Today we are more interconnected than ever. None of us is a smart as all of us. Tie in with tribes that can help you and share common values. Learn from others as they discover new tools and tricks in social networking that can help. Even the Lone Range wasn't really alone. He had Tonto by his side!

5.   **Relax.** Hey, we're all making this up as we go. I'm reminded of the first Indiana Jones movie where Karen Allen's character asked Jones what he was going to do next in the midst of another white knuckle, teeth-grinding fight. His response? "I'd don't know. I'm making this up as I go." Dealing with Social Media is like that today. In the midst of all the daily barrage of "new" step back and look at the big picture and focus on those goals you have and the "why" of your use of social media and social networking.

Allocate a specific amount of time to be on the most important social media sites for you. For professional speakers, YouTube is a key component. For healthcare professionals, staying up with others through Facebook is important to know about new advances.

For salespeople, learning about the advantages of searching through Twitter can yield real, solid bottom-line results in more sales (a nice concept in the field of selling!).

It is not about to stop. Plan your strategy and work it. Then be willing to modify as 1) you see results from your own experience, and 2) technology and the market changes. I'll make a prediction here—and I know I'm going to be right on this one. Things will Change. Yeah, big deal, Terry, you say. However, all kidding aside, plan for that and be flexible like never before. I'm talking "Gumby" kind of flexible.

Yes, it is different today and it can seem overwhelming. By following these principles you'll not only survive but your Facebook friends might just become real friends—and customers!

Now, if you'll excuse me I have a few Tweets I need to send about my new YouTube video and Facebook Fan Page along with the Linkedin Groups I monitor!

Using Twitter In Your Marketing: *Way Beyond "My Cat Is Sleeping"*

Business-Building Action From Terry Brock

In the old days (read, "last year"), many thought of Twitter as just a silly little way for kids to stay in touch and talk about "my cat is sleeping" type of messages. In other words, it was certainly not for business (at least in the minds of many people in business) and only for kids.

Things are different today. If you're not using Twitter, you are already not only passed by but you are being lapped on the track! Twitter is a force to be reckoned with in today's business environment. It can give you a decisive edge in connecting with customers, employees and fellow stakeholders. It can also help you find out the "inside scoop" on what is happening now.

How Businesses Use Twitter Today

Southwest Airlines is using it to let people know about flight changes, conditions and more. They also use it to find out what passengers are saying. If a delay or disruption occurs on a given flight, Southwest knows about it as they have dedicated people monitoring Twitter regularly.

Zappos is a great online shoe company. They monitor what customers are saying and what they want. They also use it to grab customer feedback—good and bad—and respond accordingly.

Even General (Government) Motors is using Twitter. They want to keep up with what people are saying about them and (at least in theory) help solve customer problems.

If your business is not using Twitter you are at a big disadvantage. You don't have the instant access to what is going on that is relevant to you. You won't be able to stay on top of problems and solve them before they become massive.

Filtering Twitter

A big complaint from many is that there is so much information they can't keep up with it all. I understand and agree with that. This is why experienced Twitter users (called "Twitterers") use tools to process the filtering.

TweetDeck (www.tweetdeckcom—free) is a commonly used tool to monitor key streams. You can set up a search for your company name or your competitors' names and receive notifications whenever something is said. This helps to manage the torrents of information coming through Twitter. With TweetDeck I can monitor not only important Twitter mentions but also update and monitor what is happening that is relevant for me on Facebook and Linkedin. This gives me a "command module" to keep up on the important things in my world.

HootSuite (http://hootsuite.com/dashboard—free) is another tool to monitor what is happening. It is also useful to schedule messages you'll send to others (called "Tweets"). This way you can schedule a message to go out a few times a day. Hey, the cable news networks repeat the same stories because they know their audience changes every 20 minutes—or less. Yours does too and a tool like this helps to reach more people with your message—when it is convenient for them!

Ways You Can Use Twitter In Your Marketing

There are several ways you can use Twitter but here are some that can help you immediately:

1. **Build An Audience.** This is most important as you want to build an audience of followers (that's the Twitter term for people who subscribe to your posts) who are interested in what you're doing. Have a special going on? Send a Tweet. Is there an important news event in your industry that you wrote about? Send a Tweet pointing to that article. Give lots of value and make conversation, not selling, your goal.
2. **Monitor What They Say About Your Competitors.** You need to be aware of what is happening in the world. Using Twitter is

one of the best and fastest ways to keep up with what is going on today.

3. **Become A Resource, Not A Screaming Salesperson.** One of the cardinal rules of marketing with Twitter and other Web 2.0 tools is to be a resource of information and not an annoying, pest selling stuff. Hey, there's nothing wrong with selling and I believe everyone is selling something. However, today you have to do it in a conversational, problem-solving way. Provide lots of valuable information (valuable as defined by your market) and people will want to be around you.

This is a beginning. Twitter is a serious business tool. Wade into it slowly and get familiar with the territory. You'll be glad you did. And who knows, maybe even your cat will sleep better!

Copyright (c) 2010, Terry Brock and Achievement Systems, Inc.

Terry Brock is an international marketing coach and professional speaker who helps businesses generate profitable esults. He can be reached by e-mail at terry@terrybrock.com or through his website at www.terrybrock. com. Join the Twitter adventure with Terry through his Twitter address: TerryBrock

STEPHANIE WARD

Why Facebook and LinkedIn are Good for Your Business

Have you been hearing the entire buzz about social networking? Feeling confused? Don't worry, you're not alone. The great news is that it isn't as complicated or time consuming as it may seem. Plus, it's more than just social; it's good for your business to get involved.

The list of social networking sites is long and growing. I don't want to overwhelm you so I'm only going to focus on two that are particularly suited for you as a business owner, *Facebook* and *LinkedIn*.

So why should you care? What's the big deal? Well, here are just a few reasons to enter the social networking realm:

- Gain exposure for your business that may lead to new clients or project.s
- Increase the credibility of your business (give and receive recommendations on LinkedIn, post messages on friend's pages on Facebook).
- Be connected to the people in your network in one location (OK, two if you're on both Facebook and LinkedIn).
- Re-connect with business contacts you've lost touch with (sometimes they find you, sometime you discover them).
- Meet new people and expand your business network (meet your friend's friends that you otherwise wouldn't meet).

Here's a quick overview of them (both are gratis and LinkedIn offers paid upgrade options).

Facebook:

- Informal and more social than business focused (this doesn't mean it's not good for your business).
- Almost 100 million members (according to Wikipedia).
- Anyone can ask you to be 'friends' (you don't have to accept) and you can ask anyone to be friends (they don't have to accept either).
- It is possible to share photos, videos, and add applications.
- You can join groups within the network that interest you (or make your own group).

LinkedIn:

- Business focused.
- 19 million members (according to wikipedia).
- You can only invite people you know (people whose e-mail addresses you have) and vice versa.
- It is not possible to share photos and video (only your own profile photo).
- You can join groups within the network that interest you.

To get started you just have to go to the website, sign up and follow the directions to create a profile. Because LinkedIn is mainly for business it is professional and the profile area is quite structured which makes it easy to follow.

Facebook is another story, although it does have a structured profile area, there are loads of additional features you can add to your page. When you join for business reasons be careful not to make your page too busy or too personal. You can be yourself and share your interests, just don't reveal anything you wouldn't feel comfortable sharing with a group at an in-person networking meeting.

When your profiles are finished you can start asking people to connect. The process is different for LinkedIn and Facebook but both are pretty straightforward. LinkedIn has a 'Help/FAQ' section on the website and Facebook has a 'Help' area as well (bottom right hand corner of the page).

You will learn more as you go, so just go ahead and get started. And as you meet new people you can ask them to join you on your networks. Networking, off-line or on-line, is about building relationships over time. So give first when possible, be yourself, and have fun with it.

The benefits of social networking for business owners are clear. You will be able to meet new people, build relationships with your network, improve visibility for your company, and discover new opportunities for more business. But that's not all, it's fun too. So why not get started and join the world of social networking today.

© Stephanie Ward, March 2008

Stephanie Ward is the Marketing Coach for Entrepreneurs who want to set their profits on fire! Grab your FREE copy of the special report '7 Steps to Attract More Clients in Less Time' plus business building tips, at: http://www.fireflycoaching.com

Meet Some Buddies

In case you are new to social media or are already in the system for some time, you always want to get to know certain key people who are doing exceptionally well in these social media in order to get a heads up in getting to your aim.

As the saying goes, "Birds of the same feather flock together." W.Clement Stone also puts it in another way and I quote: "Be careful with the friends you choose, for you will become like them."

So if you are sure of the kind of life you want to live, identify people who are living your dream lifestyle now and do all you can to align yourself with them. Seek them out, make friends with them, study what they are doing, model their steps and very importantly, see how you can be of help to them too in order not to come across as a greedy, selfish person who is just a go-getter but not a go-giver.

Believe me, these successful people LOVE to teach others how they managed to make such great successes as long as they see and feel that you are humble, polite, giving and ready to learn and take action.

. . . And the only easiest and cost-effective way to do this and also achieve great success at the same time in today's world (in my opinion) is through social media.

For that matter, I have put together some (not all) of my exceptional buddies in social media and some tools that will get you on the right footing.

Go through the list, do research on them through Google and find out if they are living the life you are dreaming of or the kind of people you will feel comfortable to associate with. If yes, then make friends with them right away wherever they are in social media. And don't forget to behave right and properly so that they see you as a person worth having as a friend in the first place.

Also, go through the tools and pick out the right ones that you believe will help you make the best out of social media.

THE "MUST KNOW" IN MY SOCIAL MEDIA CIRCLE:

If you are new to social media and would like to have some head-start, I would like to introduce you to some of my friends who have been providing, in my opinion, great information and advice in social media and very importantly, have made me feel at home in the cyber world. Find out about them and if they match the types of people you would like to associate with, please do not hesitate to send them a note for friendship and tell them Marjorie recommended them to you. After all, that is what networking is all about, right?! So here are . . .

My randomly selected Exceptional and Resourceful Social Networking friends:

Some of The Exceptional Lady Friends in Social Media:

Amy Wong, http://www.netdirectives.com/
Angelique Rewers, http://www.landcorporateclients.com/
Linda Claire Puig, http://www.tinyurl.com/21-6fbs
Kristin Thompson, http://www.speakservegrow.com/
Shawn Driscoll, http://yoursignatureprogram.com/info/
Chantal Beaupre, http://www.chantalbeaupre.com/
Ali Rodriguez, http://www.visionforsuccess.biz/
Murshidah Said, http://www.murshidahsaid.wordpress.com/
Wessam Mohie, http://wessammohie.com/SFBS2012/
Becky Cortino, http://www.beckycortino.info/
Laura Rubinstein, http://www.TransformYourSocialNetWorth.com
JoAnn Youngblood King, http://www.liveyourpotential.com

Kathleen Gage, http://www.themarketingmindset.com
Stephanie Ward, http://www.fireflycoaching.com
Rev. Dr. Lorraine Cohen, http://powerfull-living.biz
Mari Smith, http://marismith.com/
Nancy Marmolejo, http://www.vivavisibility.com
Denis Wakeman, http://www.boostyourvisibility.com
Lynne Klippel, http://www.businessbuildingbooks.com/
Donna Cutting, http://www.donnacutting.com/
Inez Bracy, http://overfiftyfineandfancy.com/
Therese Prentice, http://www.holisticlifestyling.com/
Walethia Aquil, http://www.graceandcharm.com/
Dr Caroline Leaf, http://www.drleaf.com/
Fabienne Fredrickson, http://clientattraction.com/
LaShanda Henry, http://www.sistasense.com/
Linda Boertjens, http://www.orangepeel.co.nz/
Donna Payne, http://thewebcoach.net/
Enyonam Gbekle, http://www.enyonamsdailydevotions.blogspot.com/
Shirley Owusu-Mensah, http://shirleyoseimensah.com/
Candace Travers, http://pollvictorytv.ning.com/
MaryEllen Tribby, http://www.workingmomsonly.com/
Eva Gregory, http://www.yourguidanceondemand.com/
Lisa Sasevich, http://www.6figureteleseminarsecrets.com/
Margaret Hampton, http://www.floridalocalseo.com/
Marci Shimoff, http://www.happyfornoreason.com/
Dr Ellie Drake, http://www.braveheartwomen.com/
Sandra Baptist, http://www.iawab.com/
Dr Sue Morter, http://www.morterinstitute.com/
Robin Fisher Roffer, http://bigfishmarketing.com/
Brenda Eason, http://www.bbon.biz/
Adela Rubio, http://enlightenedlistbuilding.com/

Some of The Exceptional Gentlemen Friends in Social Media:

Joe Sugarman, http://www.stem120.com
Paul Lawrence Vann, http://www.paullawrencevann.com/
Terry Brock, http://www.terrybrock.com/
Adam Urbanski, http://TheMarketingMentors.com/
Billy Cox, http://www.billycoxinternational.com/

Chris Brogan, http://www.chrisbrogan.com/
Dr Joe Vitale, http://www.mrfire.com/
Greg Reid, http://gregsreid.com/
Yk Amakye Ansah-Yeboah
Peter Appiah-Danquah
Forrest Anthony Knight Sr., http://newmediamarketingpros.net
Les Brown, http://www.lesbrown.com/
David Meerman Scott, http://www.webinknow.com/
Alex Karis, http://www.hurricaneofgratitude.com/
Dr Joe Rubino, http://www.selfesteemsystem.com/
Ali Kahn, http://www.advice.tv/
Augustine Blay
Herbert Mensah, http://herbertmensah.wordpress.com/
Kojo Antwi, http://www.kojoantwi.com/
Mike Berry, http://gratitude-rocks.com/
Jim Turner
Dov Baron, http://baronmastery.com/
Jerry Sam

Sonebrity™ (Social Networking Celebrity) Hall of Fame

Sonebrity™ is all about social networking people creating extraordinary impressions in Social Media in their own unique way with polish and style for a good cause. This is just the beginning. If you know any other person who deserves to be a SONEBRITY™, please do not hesitate to send me the name and reason for choosing that person at: sonebrity@ohyoubehave.com

Mensah Otabil
Mari Smith
Kathleen Gage
Kojo Antwi
Kofi Annan
Fabienne Fredrickson
Ali Brown
Alex Karis
Shirley Osei-Mensah
Natalie Regoli
Augustine Blay

Paul Lawrence Vann
Denise Wakeman
Billy Cox
Dr Caroline Leaf
Dr. Joe Vitale
Marci Shimoff
Yk Amakye Ansah-Yeboah
Peter Appiah-Danquah
Gary Vaynerchuk
Anthony Robbins
Guy Kawasaki
Seth Godin

Social Media Tools

Recommended Networking Sites for the Professional:

facebook.com
twitter.com
LinkedIn.com
Pinterest.com
Xing.com
ecademy.com
friedfeed.com
Ning.com
Instagram.com

Recommended Applications for social networking:

Facebook
Friend Finder
Podclass
vchatter—for live chatting

Twitter
TweetDeck
Twhirl
Hootsuite
Social Oomph
twellow
exectweets

Recommended social media Tools

Blogging:
Wordpress (my #1 choice)
Typepad
Blogger

Blog content sharing:
Technorati
Blog Carnival

Podcasting
Ping.fm
Cinch.fm
Tubmogul.com

RSS:
Feedburner
Friendfeed

Bookmarking tools:
Bookmarker
Sexy bookmarks
Share
Add

Shortened URL services:
bit.ly
ow.ly

Video sharing:
YouTube
Yahoo video
Viddler
Vimeo
Metacafe
Daily motion

Hulu
Blip.tv

Video with slide shows
Animoto
flixtime

Specific for Video blogging
blip.tv

Broadcasting to multiple platforms
Tubemogul
Yubby.com
blinkx.com
beet.tv

REFERENCES

Stern magazine 37/2009

AllEtiquette.com

Russell H. Conwell, *Acres of Diamonds*

Sue Fox, *Business Etiquette for Dummies*

Joseph Sugarman, *Triggers*

Terry L. Brock (2009), *Relationship Marketing: It's NOT About E-Commerce (Electronics) It's About R-Commerce (Relationships)*

Terri Morrison and Wayne A. Conaway, *Kiss, Bow, and Shake Hands*

Dr Spencer Johnson (1999), *Who moved my cheese?*

Anthony Robbins (1997), *Unlimited Power*

Dr Caroline Leaf, *Who Switched Off My Brain?*

www.netlingo.com

http://www.suemorter.com/

http://wordnetweb.princeton.edu/perl/webwn?s=blog

Marjorie Janczak

http://lass.calumet.purdue.edu/cca/mgv/index.html

http://lass.calumet.purdue.edu/cca/mgv/

http://www.geopolitics.ch/en/icgs.htm

http://crf.hudson.org/index.cfm?fuseaction=mission

http://religiousfreedom.lib.virginia.edu/universal/Dignitat.html

http://www.heise.de/tp/r4/artikel/8/8018/1.html

http://www.jite.org/documents/Vol9/JITEv9p173-181Eshet802.pdf

http://www.fastcompany.com/blog/wendy-marx/brand-u-wendy-marx/careers-facebooks-pied-piper-and-personal-branding-0

http://news.bbc.co.uk/2/hi/science/nature/1834682.stm

http://www.psychologicalscience.org/observer/getArticle.cfm?id=2010

http://center-for-nonverbal-studies.org/nvcom.htm

Aviram, R., & Eshet-Alkalai, Y. (2006). Towards a theory of digital literacy: Three scenarios for the next steps. *European Journal of Open Distance E-Learning*. Retrieved from http://www.eurodl.org/materials/contrib/2006/Aharon_Aviram.htm.

Ba, H., Tally, W., & Tsikalas, K. (2002). Investigating children's emerging digital literacies. *Journal of Technology, Learning and Assessment, 1*. Retrieved from http://www.jtla.org.

Bawden, D. (2001). Information and digital literacies: A review of concepts. *Journal of Documentation, 57*218-259.

Benjamin, W. (1994). *The work of art in the age of technical reproduction.* [Hebrew translation from German]. Tel Aviv: Teamin Publishers.

Bruce, B. C. (2003).*Literacy in the information age: Inquiries into meaning making with new technologies.* Newark, Delaware: International Reading Association.

Eshet-Alkalai, Y. (2004). Digital literacy: A conceptual framework for survival skills in the digital era. *Journal of Educational Multimedia and Hypermedia, 13,* 93-106.

Eshet-Alkalai, Y. (2008a). Humans under bombardment. *Inroads—The SIGCSE Bulletin, 39*(4), 57-61.

Eshet-Alkalai, Y., & Amichai-Hamburger, Y. (2004). Experiments with digital literacy. *Cyber Psychology and Behavior, 7,*425-434.

Eshet-Alkalai, Y., & Chajut, E. (2009). Changes over time in digital literacy. *Cyber Psychology and Behavior, 12,* 713-715. doi: 10.1089=cpb.2008.0264.

Eshet-Alkalai, Y., & Geri, N. (2007). Does the medium affect the message? The influence of text representation format on critical thinking. *Human Systems Management, 26,* 269-279.

Eshet-Alkalai, Y., & Geri, N. (2009). Congruent versus incongruent display: The effect of page layout on critical reading in print and digital formats. In Y. Eshet, A. Caspi, S.

Eden, N. Geri & Y. Yair (Eds.), *Learning in the Technological Era IV: Proceedings of the 2009 Chais Conference,* 18.2. 2009, Raanana, The Open University of Israel, pp. 73-80.

Garrison, D. R., Anderson, T., & Archer, W. (2000). Critical inquiry in a text-based environment: Computer conferencing in higher education. *The Internet and Higher Education, 2,* 85-105.

Hargittai, E. (2002). Beyond logs and surveys: In-depth measures of people's web use skills. *Journal of the American Society for Information Science and Technology, 53,* 1239-1244.

Labbo, L. D., Reinking, D., & McKenna M. C. (1998). Technology and literacy education in the next century: Exploring the connection between work and schooling. *Peabody Journal of Education, 73,* 273-289.

Shneiderman, B. (1998). *Designing the user interface.* New York: Addison Wesley.

Spiro, R. J., Feltovitch, P. L., Jacobson, M. J., & Coulson, R. L. (1991). Cognitive flexibility, constructivism and hypertext: Random access instruction for advanced knowledge acquisition in ill-structured domains. *Educational Technology, 31,* 24-33.

Tuft, E.R. (1990). *Envisioning Information.* Cheshire, CT: Graphic Press.